INFLECTI●N
POINT

An IIM Calcutta alumna, **Disha** has spent more than a decade with corporate giants such as Amazon, Paytm and Yatra, and is currently a product manager with Google India. Disha has been chosen as Young Leader by the *Economic Times*. Her published works include three books, each of which has been recognized by prominent personalities and media for their literary contributions. Her second book, *Because Life Is a Gift*, is a national bestseller and the third one, *Corporate Avatars*, is a satirical take on corporate life.

Praise for the Book

No matter what the scale and scope, and which industry your business belongs to, this book offers valuable lessons for corporate leaders of today and tomorrow.

—**Hitesh Oberoi**, CEO, InfoEdge
(Naukri, Jeevansathi, 99acres and Shiksha)

Inflection Point is an essential read to understand how some corporates and their leaders transformed their industry in one of the most challenging times of our lifetime. It also amplified the human spirit—how leading with compassion makes business sense and why doing good is good for everyone.

—**V.R. Ferose**, Senior Vice President,
SAP Labs Silicon Valley and Founder, India Inclusion Foundation

A well-articulated narrative on the struggles and triumphs of businesses and the lessons learnt during a crisis.

—**Saurabh Vashishtha**, Founder, simsim; Ex Senior Vice President, Paytm and Ex Senior Engagement Manager, McKinsey

Beat the odds as you learn from those who pivoted their business models to stem the tide.

—**Manish Amin**, CIO, Yatra

Relatable challenges, common leadership principles and lessons of a lifetime, *Inflection Point* is truly a masterstroke in leading and learning. One should never stop learning.
—**Nitin Sethi**, Vice President, Indigo

Whether you are a student, a CEO, or an entrepreneur in the making, *Inflection Point* will coach and inspire you to jump into real and quick action. It's a book for all heroes this world is waiting for.

—**Durga Shakti Nagpal**, IAS Officer

Authentic and engaging...great first-person accounts of leading during one of the biggest crises of the century!

—**Dhruv Dhanraj Bahl**, CEO, BharatPe

Disha has interviewed a diverse group of leaders to remind us what courageous leadership looks like. These case studies demystify leadership during times of crisis and bring out the simple steps that any leader can take to make a difference.
—**Sumit Gupta**, Leadership Coach, Deploy Yourself

Inflection Point comes at a time when traditional practices can no longer serve businesses. As leaders are pushed to rethink and create a new future, Disha is bringing their real-life work to the audience through well-researched stories. Timely and authentic!

—**Nistha Tripathi**, bestselling author of *No Shortcuts*

INFLECTI●N POINT

Leadership Lessons
from Turbulent Times

Disha

RUPA

Published by
Rupa Publications India Pvt. Ltd 2021
7/16, Ansari Road, Daryaganj
New Delhi 110002

Sales centres:
Allahabad Bengaluru Chennai
Hyderabad Jaipur Kathmandu
Kolkata Mumbai

Copyright © Disha 2021

All rights reserved.
No part of this publication may be reproduced, transmitted,
or stored in a retrieval system, in any form or by any means,
electronic, mechanical, photocopying, recording or otherwise,
without the prior permission of the publisher.

The views and opinions expressed in this book are
the author's own and the facts are as reported by her
which have been verified to the extent possible,
and the publishers are not in any way liable for the same.

ISBN: 978-93-90547-82-1

First impression 2021

10 9 8 7 6 5 4 3 2 1

The moral right of the author has been asserted.

Printed at HT Media Ltd, Greater Noida

This book is sold subject to the condition that it shall not,
by way of trade or otherwise, be lent, resold, hired out, or otherwise
circulated, without the publisher's prior consent, in any form of
binding or cover other than that in which it is published.

CONTENTS

Author's Note   vii

1. ITC Limited   1
2. Manipal Hospitals   11

Lesson 1: Nimbleness

3. Urban Company (aka UrbanClap)   22
4. Zerodha   30

Lesson 2: Thinking Customer Backwards

5. Delhi Police   42
6. Delhi Government Administration   49

Lesson 3: Power of Communication

7. ACT   60
8. TUI Group   69

Lesson 4: Importance of a Business Continuity Plan

9. Dunzo   80
10. IXIGO   87

Lesson 5: Employee Well-Being

11. Family of Disabled   98
12. Brigade Metropolis RWA   105

Lesson 6: Rising Above Self-interest

13. YourNest Venture Capital	115
14. myResQR.life	122

Lesson 7: Being Open to Fail

15. NamaStay Away	131
16. Landmark	138

Lesson 8: Innovation

17. Cafe Delhi Heights	150
18. 360 Realtors	159

Lesson 9: Being in Unison with Government Guidelines

19. Shapoorji Pallonji Group	171
20. Emerson	179

Lesson 10: Importance of Technology

Conclusion	190
Acknowledgements	191
Index	193

AUTHOR'S NOTE

On 30 January 2020, I was on a plane, on my way back from Tokyo via Hong Kong, when I heard the word 'Coronavirus' for the first time. At the Hong Kong airport, everyone was wearing masks. No one knew then that it would turn into a pandemic so large in its scope and so grim in its shadow that it would change our lives forever. As I finish writing this book, several months have passed since that day in January. Our routine lives and habits have changed forever. The way we eat, play, work and live has altered. The resultant lockdowns across the globe have brought national economies to a standstill. Salary and job cuts are happening throughout the world. 'Lives versus livelihood' is a constant debate. No one living in these times has experienced a crisis that can be remotely equated to this one. And things are still unfolding!

We are not going out to eat, but cooking at home; we now prefer services being offered/delivered at home, rather than stepping out; high-speed internet has become a necessity to work seamlessly from home and masks have become the new fashion statement and they are here to stay. All these changes in our behaviour are shaping the way different industries are leading their way through the crisis and changing their core strategy. COVID-19 has not just affected our everyday lives, it has impacted every sphere of the corporate world too.

The pandemic has had a varied impact on several industries across the globe, which have suddenly found their revenue nosedive to zero or even turn negative. For instance, the travel industry, which relied heavily on people physically moving around, had to refund future bookings. Physical events and movie ticketing in the entertainment industry fall in the same category, and there is still no clarity on when revenue generation would start again. Then there are industries that fall in the bucket of 'putting off for the future'; for instance, people have been putting off their visit to the dentist for a time when the crisis has eased. What this entails for such industries is that their present revenues are being shifted to the future. The immediate focus for such industries is cash conservation.

Another behaviour that the pandemic has encouraged is hoarding; whether it's toilet paper in the western countries or Maggi noodles in India, we all have been guilty of hoarding, at least earlier in the lockdown period. What it has meant for industries selling such products—as long as they are essentials and non-perishable items—is that their future revenues have been brought forward and at some point in the future, the present-day spends may impact the future spends.

On the other end, being stuck at home and having a lot more time at hand, people are taking up new hobbies such as cooking, gardening and other isolation-friendly activities or renewing old, somewhere-lost interests. Baking banana bread has become a huge trend. Those providing virtual classes for such activities or those in the business of the required raw materials are attracting significant discretionary spends towards their products and services. This is new revenue for the companies but one that may not sustain once people begin to step out for leisure and entertainment.

And then there are big winners in this crisis. Industries such as video conferencing, online grocers, digital payments and so on have seen a huge spike in adoption and reached levels that would have otherwise taken them months or even years. These are likely fundamental customer behaviour changes and are expected to continue even when the crisis has eased. These industries are not just making a lot of revenue during the crisis; even when the pandemic is somewhat over, the 'new normal' of these industries is likely to be at a higher level than the pre-pandemic times. These industries are mostly constrained on their supply side to handle the exponential growth in demand.

When I set out to write this book, I myself wanted to learn how business leaders are thinking and organizing themselves through the crisis. A few years down the line, the crisis of today and the leadership and business lessons drawn from it, will be taught as crisis management case studies in B-schools. Which of these lessons will be permanent armours for future leaders in dealing with any crisis? And do the learnings differ depending on which side of the revenue curve a company finds itself in? Does leadership need to be reactive?

Inflection Point is based on first-person accounts of top leaders across different industries on the emerging challenges and opportunities that we are faced with in this new world. The leaders share candid accounts about how their industries and their organizations have been impacted by this pandemic and what has been their top priority in these trying times. Each story has valuable leadership lessons—lessons that will remain true for any future crisis. There are also stories of how the pandemic is impacting the leaders at a personal level; how they are balancing employee well-being and investor interests. The diversity of the industries brings in many dimensions in these engaging conversations.

What you read in this book is not in-your-face dos and don'ts. This is not a preachy self-help book or a manual on how to navigate your way through a crisis. The leadership lessons are far more subtle and concealed in the actions of these leaders.

What makes the book special and unique is that the organizations in focus here, despite being so different—not just in being from different industries but also because of how varied they are in terms of their lifespan, scale and scope—the underlying thinking of the leaders is tied together and coherent in its messages. A 155-year-old conglomerate is leading in the same way as a new start-up. A fashion firm is sharing the same leadership principles as a hospital. A leader whose customers are in the Indian market and another whose customers are global, are thinking alike. A not-for-profit is thinking the same way as an organization measured by its stakeholder value.

I am thus convinced that these are the lessons that one can apply in leading through any crisis and not just a pandemic.

The book is a result of many hours of reading, phone calls and healthy discussions between these business leaders and me. I appreciate the research material the companies provided me with, and also the phone calls and video discussions with many team members to get their diverse perspectives. I appreciate the time invested by them to patiently edit the drafts with me. Especially when one is facing tough situations at work, carving out this time is extremely challenging.

I have consciously tried to minimize my personal interpretations of a story and represented them from these leaders' points of view. The leadership snippets interspersed with these stories tie the common threads together.

Given the rapid change in our everyday world, by the time you finish reading this book, a lot might have changed. Worst-case scenario, some of these companies may probably find themselves in the midst of a survival crisis. Despite what happens, the leadership lessons that are valid today will remain so in the future as well. And of course, one can learn more from failures, if any.

I am a corporate professional. Writing is my passion. I write because I am touched, moved and inspired by people around me. I learnt a lot through these leaders and hope you do too, as you read, pause and reflect on their journeys.

∼

The thought of writing this book occurred to me in March 2020 and some of the earliest interviews were conducted as early as April. I kept in touch with the representatives of these organizations and made revisions to the stories over time. However, the journey of a manuscript, in its raw form, till it goes to print, is a journey of a few months, too.

The world today is more dynamic than ever. It is possible that some parts of the interviews seem a little dated. The story of each organization may have evolved since the time I last interviewed these leaders. I do not claim to present the most updated picture of an organization. These stories are set in the midst of a crisis, which will, hopefully, become a thing of the past. And while I have done extensive secondary research for each of the stories, I do not claim to verify every word as told to me by the esteemed representatives of the organization.

1

ITC LIMITED

ITC Limited is one of India's foremost private-sector companies and a diversified conglomerate with businesses spanning from fast-moving consumer goods (FMCG), hotels, paperboards and packaging, to agri business and information technology. The company is acknowledged as one of the country's most valuable business corporations, with a market capitalization of nearly US$35 billion (as on 30 June 2020) and a gross sales value of US$10.74 billion (as on 31 March 2020).[1] ITC was ranked as India's most admired company, according to a survey conducted by Fortune India, in association with Hay Group. Established in 1910, it completed 100 years in 2010 and is part of the Forbes 2000 list. A global exemplar in sustainability, ITC is the only enterprise in the world of comparable dimensions to be carbon-positive, water-positive and solid waste recycling-positive for over a decade now.

Over the last decade, ITC's new consumer goods businesses have established a vibrant portfolio of 25 world-class Indian brands that create and retain value. Its superior FMCG brands, including Aashirvaad, Sunfeast, YiPPee!, Bingo!, B Natural, ITC Master Chef, Fabelle, Sunbean, Fiama, Engage, Vivel, Savlon, Classmate, Paperkraft, Mangaldeep, Aim and others have garnered encouraging consumer franchise within a short span of time.

The competitiveness of ITC's diverse businesses rest on the strong foundations of institutional strengths derived from its deep consumer insights, cutting-edge research & development (R&D), differentiated product development capacity, brand-building capability, world-class

---

[1] https://en.wikipedia.org/wiki/ITC_Limited

manufacturing infrastructure, extensive rural linkages, efficient trade marketing and distribution network and dedicated human resources. ITC's ability to leverage internal synergies residing across its diverse businesses lends a unique source of competitive advantage to its products and services.

ITC's 'Nation First: Sab Saath Badhein' (Nation First: Let's All Grow Together) philosophy underlines its core belief in building a globally competitive and profitable Indian enterprise that makes an exemplary contribution to creating larger societal value. As a company that is deeply rooted in the Indian ethos, ITC is inspired by the opportunity to serve larger national priorities.

∼

The greatest danger in times of turbulence is not the turbulence; it is to act with yesterday's logic.

—Peter Drucker

We have always known that everything we use and consume are not essentials, but it took the pandemic for this terminology of essential and non-essential items, and the difference between them to really seep in. Over a period of time, as the lockdown progressed, we all began to understand this distinction better. We now know that grocery is an essential need. Even before the government announced the first lockdown in March 2020, many of my friends suggested I stock up groceries at least for two months. The pandemic created a sense of immense uncertainty and gave rise to an urge to hoard.

As I tapped on the grocery app on my phone, adding one item after the other to the cart, I thought about how the FMCG sector was going to operate. How will they run factories in a pandemic? What about their raw material supplies? How will they manage distribution, especially the interstate movements?

However, a couple of months into the lockdown, I realized that when it came to the availability of household essentials, there had been no issue whatsoever. Despite intermittent news of vehicles being held at state borders and drivers finding it difficult with the roadside food outlets closed, FMCG companies ensured a continuous supply of groceries into our homes.

As I began narrowing down my choices of companies I could reach out to, I was keen on having an Indian brand and so, I picked one that has created multiple food brands in the FMCG space. The company that was once singled out for its cigarette business has come to have more than 60 per cent of its business from other diverse verticals. ITC has 160 factories across 130 cities. With presence in 21 states and 220 districts, the company's agri business is spread far and wide. With more than 100 hotels in over 70 destinations, ITC's brand of premium hotels has set new standards of excellence in the hospitality industry. At a personal level, ITC's best recall in my household is with the Aashirvaad atta, YiPPee noodles, Savlon antiseptic, Shower to Shower talcum, Fiama shampoo and Classmate notebooks.

I was filled with gratitude and humility when, despite a demanding corporate life, Anil Rajput, head of Corporate Affairs at ITC Limited, agreed to talk to me. Anil's job entails public policy advocacy related to ITC's business verticals across its hotel business, FMCG, paper and paperboards, printing and packaging, cigarettes and agri business.

To interview a person of his stature was overwhelming. How can any recounting do justice to 44 years of experience with ITC? I was curious to know if he had seen a crisis of this magnitude in his many years of experience, where he would have witnessed many challenges.

'There has been nothing like this in the last 100 years,' Anil says. 'The closest events of this nature are the World Wars. This pandemic, however, is even more crippling for the global economy and its end is not yet in sight, because we are fighting an invisible enemy. Today, the world is a lot more interconnected and interdependent than it was during the World Wars. Therefore, economic impact would be more severe and likely to last much longer. We can already see how this pandemic is impacting the health, well-being and livelihoods of society, and it is difficult to see the light at the end of this tunnel.'

As early as February 2020, the growing concern of coronavirus was felt across the globe, and by March, it had become apparent that India wouldn't remain unaffected by it. The only variable was the degree of impact.

'In India, the growing concern for the pandemic became apparent in early March, which is when we started to prepare for a potential impact on our ecosystem. Our businesses and value chains create sustainable livelihoods for more than 6 million people, a majority of whom represent the poorest in rural India. Almost 34,000 people are directly employed by the group. When the first signs of the pandemic emerged, our topmost priority was to ascertain employee safety.'

Like several other conscientious businesses, ITC decided to take proactive measures. As Anil tells us, 'ITC is known to be an enterprise with a human face. Even before the COVID-19 crisis, our chairman, Sanjiv Puri, put the wheels in motion to ensure the health and safety of all employees. Without delay, the human resource (HR) department was asked to develop appropriate advisories—dos and don'ts—for all employees, particularly for those working on the front line. Mr Puri ensured that ITC's support model addressed holistic employee well-being, both physical and mental. Wherever it was possible to work remotely, infrastructure was created accordingly.'

ITC's next priority was to keep business operations running, with the right safety protocols. The company was aware that the COVID crisis was going to cause a disruption in its supply chains and hence needed to prepare for that. There was also a need to ensure that the supplies of the FMCG essentials did not fall short.

'We ensured that our factories were set up with all safety protocols. Our learning and development department needed to be agile and train our distributed manpower on social distancing. Our workers were provided additional incentives and meals and all the safety equipment they needed to take care of themselves while they went about their work. We were in a dialogue at various levels with government authorities to ensure that workers had access to come to work. Our logistic partners were also able to work seamlessly to meet the national call of duty.'

Doing this at the scale that ITC operates was no mean feat. Even within the FMCG business, different brands anticipated varied impact of the pandemic. While the demand for products such as atta (wheat flour), noodles, biscuits, chips, juices, etc. was expected to soar, the sale of products such as Classmate notebooks, chewing gums, etc. were expected to be under pressure, at least in the short term. In its most rigorous form, the lockdown allowed the manufacture, distribution and sale of only essential commodities. Since cigarettes fell in the category of non-essential items, smokers did not have easy access to them and, this in turn, led to revenue shortfall. The key was to focus on customers' needs. For example, the company reprioritized a newly commissioned perfume manufacturing facility in Himachal Pradesh for the production of sanitizers sold under the Savlon brand.

'The key was to focus on customers' needs. Balancing was critical. Given the social distancing requirements, we could not operate our factories at full manpower. This required refashioning the processes to ensure that we maximize our capacity utilization while staying within government regulations. COVID-19 provided a new opportunity for the company in the area of hand sanitizers, and our research and development (R&D) and product development teams were quick to seize this opportunity.'

ITC's FMCG business innovated at all levels. A typical product launch, from conceptualization to launch, normally takes around six to seven months. Savlon's brand of sanitizers and disinfectant spray was launched within a month of its conceptualization—that too when teams were just coming to terms with the new reality of the world.

Keeping affordability in mind, the company launched hand sanitizer sachets at 50 paise and slashed the price of its existing units from ₹77 to ₹27.

'Sanitizers are our armour in this battle. What is the use of production if they are not affordable to millions of customers who need it?'

To avoid multiple top-ups, the company came out with larger packaging for its food products.

Innovation and new partnerships happened on the distribution side too.

'COVID-19 restrictions forced us to innovatively look at our distribution channels to reach customers in the quickest manner by delayering our supply chain systems. We looked at more avenues of hyperlocal deliveries and partnered with Amway, Domino's, Swiggy, Zomato and Dunzo. We also started delivering through our own ITC stores web portal. The "Store on Wheels" initiative has partnered with apps such as mygate to directly send an array of ITC products in trucks to residential societies that have sufficient demand to make the operations cost-effective. This is a win-win proposition for customers and ITC, the former do not need to step out to get their groceries. Our diverse range of products ensures we have one for every need.'

At a time when companies were undercommitting, ITC's ad campaign on an assured supply of YiPPee noodles created a euphoria for the home-alone, work-stressed customers. YiPPee registered growth during the two months since the pandemic.

While prioritizing short-term needs of essential items, the company also continued to work actively on its mid-to-long term strategy. Be it the acquisition of Sunrise Foods to fortify its spices business or extension of the Aashirvaad brand to include ghee, pouch milk, paneer and pouch curd, ITC never lost sight of the verticals which now were an even bigger opportunity. The company expects growth in health, wellness and hygiene products and is focusing on innovations across all its verticals.

Even before the Prime Minister's push for Make in India and self-reliance, ITC's mantra has been Nation First. Most of its raw materials are locally sourced. In the ₹7,400-crore agarbatti (incense stick) business, ITC's Mangaldeep brand holds a significant share. For the agarbatti business, India is importing raw batti (bamboo sticks coated with masala) from China and Vietnam, resulting in job creation outside the country. This is because production of raw batti is primarily dependent on the plantation of a specific species of bamboo, which is currently unavailable in India. To be self-reliant in the production of raw batti, there is a need to plant the right type of bamboo in India. ITC is working with the farming community in the Northeast to ensure India's self-reliance in the production of raw materials for agarbatti and creating new jobs opportunities in the country.

'ITC is an organization with an Indian soul and will continue to work for the benefit of its citizens. We are always exploring avenues that can create more livelihood opportunities in the hinterlands of the country.'

Shifting gears on other businesses, particularly the cigarette business, a money-spinner for ITC, is currently on a slow burner. ITC's agri business has been constrained in the supplies of commodities in the market. Mandis have been closed, labour for harvesting is hard to come by, farmers are not able to protect the crops and trucks are stuck. The recently announced reforms for governance and administration of the agriculture sector, including amendments to the Essential Commodities Act, reforms in agricultural marketing and risk mitigation through predictable prices will empower farmers, strengthen agri-food processing linkages and enable demand-driven value-added agriculture.

'The policymakers, especially in the agri space, were very quick to respond to the needs of the farming community and made sweeping changes, which will not only provide relief in the short run, but will have transformative impacts on the lives of farmers in the years to come. The company's institutional capabilities help as the company constantly engages with farmers and labourers at the grass-roots level on one hand and district administrations and the state and central governments on the other. ITC is also making focused efforts to educate farmers and their families to adopt preventive measures to contain the spread of COVID-19 in their communities. The agri business is also leveraging mobile technologies such as ITC e-Choupal 4.0 and local field staff strength to ensure continuity of farming. Such initiatives hand-hold the farmers so that they can continue with their best practices by deploying relevant technology, with safety measures.'

ITC's hotel business had also come to a standstill during the initial months of the pandemic. Only five of the over hundred ITC hotels were operational, that too as quarantine facilities or reserved for stranded guests. It will be long before the situation improves and the group is taking innovative measures to keep its customers engaged.

'ITC is proud to present the #5StarKitchen, a cooking show that for the first time brings together the acclaimed chefs of ITC Hotels to your TV screens, with some amazing recipes. The show commenced on 23 May 2020 and is being telecast on 33 Star channels and Hotstar every weekend for six weeks. We are also bringing our favourite food to the comfort and safety of our homes through tie-up with hyperlocal players via the 5 Star Kitchen. To prioritize our employees' well-being, we have started several skill development programmes through digital platforms, which are processing salaries well ahead of time.'

While managing a company at this scale, with diverse businesses, stakeholders can take all of one's priorities, but ITC has not lost sight of its role in the community.

'Today, the nation is faced with an unprecedented challenge. ITC set up a ₹150-crore contingency fund to address and help manage the challenges arising out of this adversity. This initial fund has been utilized primarily to provide relief to the vulnerable and most economically backward sections of society, who have been the worst hit by the pandemic and faced significant disruption to their livelihoods. ITC pledged ₹100 crore to the PM CARES Fund, a humble contribution to the government's efforts in mitigating the crisis. The group has also contributed ₹27 crore to the chief ministers' relief funds across states. We have handed over a 30-bed hospital to the district administration of Haridwar to provide immediate care during COVID-19. The company is working closely with local administrations of 23 states across the country to provide essential commodities, especially to those in distress, including migrant labourers. A range of food products have been donated to district administrations, police administration, the railways and several non-governmental organizations (NGOs). These include 17 lakh packets of noodles, 32 lakh packets of biscuits, 22 lakh packs of fruit juices, 7 lakh kg of atta, 16 lakh packets of snacks, 7 lakh packs of milk shakes and 4.5 lakh bars of chocolates. Given the importance of protecting health and hygiene in fighting the COVID menace, ITC has also distributed over 28 lakh pieces of soap to health centres, hospitals and police stations, a lakh masks to front-line workers and also provided 3,000 personal protective equipment (PPEs).

ITC's Foods Division has extended support to children and senior citizens by sending food supplies across the country through its 'Aashirvaad Box of Hope' and 'Sunfeast Box of Happiness' initiatives. Similar boxes were also provided to workers of outsourced manufacturing units. Over 100,000 boxes have been delivered to date. Over 3.5 lakh meals have been cooked in ITC hotel's kitchens and provided to migrant workers and needy people across the country.

Jelimals, the confectionery brand from ITC, has come forward with an initiative to create awareness amongst children about the five steps to prevent the spread of COVID-19, as recommended by the World Health Organization (WHO). The brand teamed up with Chhota Bheem, the animation character, to bring out the "Do the 5" song[1], which is modelled on these five steps.'

Underlying all of the challenges and the response lies the core belief that agility and innovation are the key driving factors for any organization in these times. Until the last-mile consumer, the last-mile worker and the last-mile supplier or partner is not safe and financially sound, the job is not done.

---

[1] https://www.youtube.com/watch?v=3WDGv5uaaUA

'We are constantly adapting our business models and trying to stay ahead of the curve, while staying true to our mission and priority of offering our customers the best in-class products and services.'

About Anil Rajput

Anil Rajput is Senior Vice President (Corporate Affairs) at ITC Ltd and Non-Executive Director, International Travel House.

Anil joined ITC in 1976 in the Finance function. At the age of 27, he assumed charge as General Manager, travel. In this role, Anil laid a strong foundation for ITC's domestic network across India. In 1989, he moved back to the Hotels division of ITC and was assigned the responsibility of working on new projects as Divisional Project Controller.

Subsequently, he was promoted as Vice President (Project, Finance and Development). Anil has been instrumental in various hotel projects: ITC Kakatiya (Hyderabad), ITC Rajputana (Jaipur), ITC Sonar Bangla (Kolkata), and ITC Grand Maratha and ITC Grand Central (Mumbai), to name a few.

In 2003, he moved to ITC's Corporate Affairs function as Vice President (Corporate Affairs). In 2007, he took over as Senior Vice President (Corporate Affairs) and played a key role in the 13 verticals that ITC has built over the years in the regulatory and policy framework.

Besides his role at ITC, Anil is also the chairman, ASSOCHAM National Council on Advertising, Marketing Brand Promotion and Protection; chairman, FICCI CASCADE (Committee on Anti-Smuggling and Counterfeiting); and non-official member, Managing Body of Indian Red Cross Society (Delhi branch).

2

MANIPAL HOSPITALS

A pioneer in healthcare, Manipal Hospitals is among the largest hospital networks in India, serving over 2 million patients annually. Its focus is to develop an affordable tertiary care multispecialty healthcare framework through its entire multispecialty delivery spectrum and further extend it to homecare. With its flagship quaternary care facility located in Bengaluru, seven tertiary care, five secondary care and two primary care clinics spread across India and abroad, Manipal Hospitals successfully operates and manages 5,900 beds across 15 hospitals. It provides comprehensive curative and preventive care for a multitude of patients from across the globe. Manipal Hospitals has a one-day care clinic in Lagos, Nigeria too and is the first in India to be awarded accreditation by the Association for the Accreditation of Human Research Protection Programs, Inc. (AAHRPP) for ethical standards in clinical research activities. It is also an ISO: 9001-certified hospital since 2003 and has been accredited by the National Accreditation Board for Testing and Calibration Laboratories (NABL) and the National Accreditation Board for Hospitals & Healthcare Providers (NABH) as well. It is also one of the most respected hospital companies in India and the most patient-recommended hospital in India by consumer survey.[1]

∼

---

[1] 'Bangalore: Manipal Hospital Most Patient-friendly in India Survey,' DajiWorld, 11 February 2008, http://www.daijiworld.com/news/newsDisplay.aspx?newsID=43397, last accessed on 9 December 2020.

Take care of the patient and everything else will follow.

—Dr Thomas Frist

Coming from the software industry, and not having anyone among my family and friends working in the healthcare sector, my opinions and beliefs about this sector have been formed based on what I have seen and read in the media. My limited understanding was that hospitals must be bustling with business and raking in a lot of money since the pandemic hit the country. I heard about hospitals turning back patients for fear of them being infected. And I began to feel a certain degree of discomfort about featuring one of them in this book.

Spending an hour with Dilip Jose, managing director and Chief Executive Officer (CEO) of Manipal Health Enterprises, changed my perspective and gave me a lot of food for thought. From Dilip, I learnt how, contrary to my belief, most private hospitals saw a sharp decline in their revenues. And unless the government provides immediate support to this sector, several hospitals facing a severe cash crunch may have to eventually shut down.

Dilip tells me how the lockdown affected Manipal Hospitals—as it did other businesses in the healthcare sector.

'A lot of our patients come not just from the nearby areas, but also from other districts and states. In addition, there is international medical travel; in fact, close to 10 per cent of our revenue is from overseas patients. With the pausing of both international and domestic travel, many of these patients could no longer access our hospitals. In the early stages of lockdown, people were too scared to come out of their homes and even the local public transport was stalled. During April, our revenue was 30 per cent that of pre-COVID times.'

Private hospitals received instruction from the government to pause all 'non-essential procedures'. I wondered how a hospital could have services that are 'non-essential', but there are indeed, as Dilip explained to me.

'Many corrective or cosmetic procedures are not so time sensitive. Patients who need to consult the dermatology, ophthalmology or dental departments can sometimes wait a little longer. People were wary of visiting hospitals for fear of coming in contact with a COVID-infected patient. I myself needed to undergo an orthopaedic implant removal surgery, but since this had no negative impact on my health, I postponed my procedure till after the lockdown.'

Even though the outpatient footfall decreased, only those who were very sick and could not defer seeing a doctor visited the OPDs (outpatients departments). As Dilip tells me, 'Against 1/10th of the outpatients who needed to be hospitalized earlier, this ratio shot up to as high as 25–30 per cent.'

Manipal Hospitals rolled out tele-consultation with the objective of serving patients who could not physically come to the hospital. Speaking on how this is going to complement the physical infrastructure of the hospital, Dilip talks about the long-term usage of tele-medicine: 'Not only is tele-consultation a great way to reach out to patients who cannot physically come to our hospitals, it is also extremely useful for second opinions, follow-up consultations and where the symptoms can be verbally or visually assessed. We integrated tele-consultation on our patient application and saw an increased adoption of this channel. While on one hand, the need of social distancing significantly increases the need of physical space or curtails the maximum number of patients in the OPD; tele-consultation provides an alternative to serve the same number of patients per day.'

Any walk-in patient in a hospital could be COVID-positive. Even if the hospital was not a COVID treatment centre/hospital and all the staff needed to do was to redirect the patient to one that was, they still needed to ensure that the staff's safety was not compromised. Also, high-risk patients, especially those coming in for dialysis, chemotherapy and cardiac treatments, needed to be protected from any chance of acquiring the infection while in the hospital.

There was also the need to be prepared for the pandemic, in

case the numbers exceeded what the government hospitals could support. To be approved/licensed to conduct COVID testing, Manipal Hospitals, tells Dilip, needed setting up of a biosafety level-2 infrastructure, one that was thus far only needed in research laboratories. The hospital also needed the right equipment, people training, protective equipment and protocols in place.

'We set up dedicated fever clinics, which had entrances separate from the main buildings. We stocked up the safety gears, even buying them at higher than market prices. Our procurement team made all the sourcing contracts to ensure that the hospital did not run out of safety equipment.

Right from putting on the PPE suit to the protocols to be followed in case we suspected someone in the staff was infected, we trained our staff, conducted several mock drills and institutionalized regular audits in all our hospitals.

'Extra sterilization, setting up of isolation wards, staff rotation and quarantine, responsible waste disposal and comprehensive disinfection were key areas of attention. Sample testing was done and the hospitals were calibrated against those tests.

'As of now, four of our hospitals are doing the testing. As of 25 June, Manipal Hospitals group has a dedicated isolation and treatment facility in Karnataka.'

Talking on how the hospital is keeping the doctors and front-line staff engaged, Dilip tells me how he has been conducting regular town halls with all the hospitals: 'These are tough times for our staff. Be it the cleaning staff or the nurse or the doctor or even the security personnel, everyone is under tremendous stress. They hear about cases of medical staff getting infected in other hospitals and are concerned not just for themselves but their families as well. We have staff who have elderly parents and young kids at home and these people do not want to go home in the fear of exposing them to the virus. There are accounts of the medical staff being discriminated against by their landlords, neighbours and friends. This is not just a financial or a business crisis, but one where the entire humanity is being tested.

'A reason I delayed in giving you an interview was because the last few weeks have been very intense and stressful and the priority was internal communication and engagement. The heads of each of our hospitals are making themselves accessible 24×7 to the staff. Regular visits and conversations with the staff, reinforcing the safety protocols has been the top agenda for all the individual leaders as well as for the group. The staff is also guided on the nutrient needs to keep themselves healthy.

'Fatigue is now setting in and it is all the more crucial for us to keep our staff consciously aware of the protocols for their safety. There is also a lot of cross-institutional knowledge-sharing and learning. Network of doctors, management staff and industry peers are conducting formal and informal sessions and brainstorming to deal with the crisis. While there are top-down directives at the Centre and state levels and regulations change quite frequently, the industry recognizes the need to be mindful of the current situation and work as one unit rather than a fragmented response.'

There has been a lot of misinformation related to COVID. Dilip believes that hospitals play a critical role in curtailing this.

'Through our social media channels, our doctors come and bust the myths related to the virus and its treatment. To give you an example, patients who needed chemotherapy or dialysis were delaying these procedures. We constantly communicated to them the hazards of doing so and assured them of their safety. We have also been actively blogging and spreading accurate information amongst our patients.

'At the same time, work from home (WFH) and a sedentary lifestyle are leading to varied health problems. Our doctors are constantly writing about lifestyle practices to be followed, especially due to the possibility of the situation stretching further. From educating people on the need to wear masks to other lifestyle risks they need to be mindful of, we are in the front and centre of dealing with the repercussions of the new normal.'

Hospital and healthcare business are people and capex intensive.

The expectation from and the need to have private hospitals that are fully equipped to respond to the pandemic has led to higher overheads and fixed costs. For the same number of patients, more manpower is needed considering a team of healthcare professionals may have to be off for 14 days of quarantine in rotation. Most hospitals are absorbing much of the additional costs at the moment so as to shield COVID patients from further expenses. There are also government directives to cap the cost of tests and treatment.

Coupled with the drop in revenues, it is impacting not only the profit and loss (P&L) but cash flows as well. Many have managed by cutting expenses to only bare essentials, deferring payments, additional borrowings and even slashing payments to doctors and employees.

Most government hospitals are also incurring huge expenses, but they can mobilize resources from other areas. However, private hospitals don't have that avenue and are left to fend for themselves in tackling the crisis on the front line. The staff of these hospitals are grappling with fear and apprehension, even as the hospitals themselves have to deal with significantly increased expenses and dwindling revenue.

Speaking of some immediate to mid-term measures that the group is taking and is recommending the government, Dilip says: 'This is a good time for us to take a hard look at our costs and look for efficiency. For example, automation of financial accounting can go a long way in efficient and real-time management of cash flows. This is a priority that the top financial leaders of the hospital are focusing on.

'At the same time, the government should give priority sector status to healthcare and push banks to lend to this sector at a lower rate of interest. Private healthcare is one of the top five sectors employing people in the country and most of the capacity in the country in healthcare has come through the private sector. Around 60 per cent of the hospitals in the country, 60 per cent of beds in hospitals and 70 per cent of specialist doctors are in private healthcare.

'We are hoping there can be a greater degree of public–private partnerships (PPP), which has never been seen before, as we look to win against this pandemic. The government and banks should help finance our fixed costs, at least for the next two quarters, through interest-free loans. Overdue amounts from state and central government schemes which we have been supporting such as the Ex-servicemen Contributory Health Scheme (ECHS), Central Government Health Scheme (CGHS) and local state government schemes, and dues from the government insurance companies should be immediately paid. Hospitals should get refunds of all statutory dues such as income tax refunds.

'We also propose that tax deducted at source (TDS) on hospital dues should not be deducted as this leads to working capital getting stuck. This capital can be utilized for supporting our patients and healthcare front-line workers. Any loss due to subsidized COVID-19 testing or treatment should be funded by the government within 30 days of discharge or bill closure.'

Healthcare has been heavily underinvested and the public spend is less than 1 per cent of the country's gross domestic product (GDP). As we think of building highways and airports, we should also be thinking of investing in hospitals, medical infrastructure and research. In the Kuala Lumpur branch of the group, the government supported 25 per cent of the staff salaries. The same is happening in hospitals in the US to support their efforts to deal with the pandemic, but no such impetus has been provided so far to the private hospitals in India. India imports almost 69 per cent of its active pharmaceutical ingredients (APIs) from China. This needs to change. Suspension of medical visas was done as a stopgap arrangement. The government needs to open up medical tourism as soon as possible; else, the other countries where it is open may end up gaining a long-term advantage.

India needs to change its attitude to the healthcare sector and give it the priority and urgency it deserves.

About Dilip Jose

Dilip Jose is the managing director and Chief Executive Officer (CEO), Manipal Health Enterprises Pvt. Ltd (Manipal Hospitals), an integrated hospital services system with 15 hospitals in India and abroad, and over 6,000 beds under management. He has over 28 years of experience in various sectors and across functional areas. In healthcare, where he has spent the last 16 years, his previous assignment was as Group CEO of CARE Hospitals, where he was managing a network of tertiary care facilities. Prior to that, he was the regional director with Fortis Healthcare, heading their operations in South India. Preceding that, he held leadership positions in the areas of medical and paramedical education as well as tertiary healthcare delivery. Before his move to the healthcare sector, Dilip spent about 12 years in various roles in corporate finance and strategy.

LESSON 1

NIMBLENESS

COVID-19 has delivered a crash course in agility for organizations of all stripes.

Ever since the first case was reported, every day has been a roller-coaster ride. Situations on the ground have evolved rapidly.

A week before, leaders were checking the sales numbers and reviewing their 2020 plans. A week later, supply chains were disrupted and businesses asked to temporarily shut shop until further notice. A day before, all our employees were safe. A day later, an entire department got infected. The time horizon of major events like a business shutting down or a business needing to change its business model was severely shortened.

As Krishan Singh, CEO, TUI India, said, 'If you did not have to change your contingency action plan within a week, you were lucky.'

The ground realities are still rapidly evolving. If anything, this crisis has taught us the importance of being nimble in a crisis.

In a crisis situation, dealing with uncertainty needs less planning, more execution. Each story stresses on the fact that this is not the time to draw a product road map, a five-year vision or long-term strategies. Leaders are embracing speed, and mitigating the short- to mid-term consequences to stabilize the situation and stay afloat.

South Korea's rapid response to the pandemic may be an exemplary demonstration of the principles of effective crisis management. The country had apparently started to stockpile coronavirus testing kits long before an outbreak had occurred on its own shores, allowing testing of 10,000 people a day when the infection rate started to climb, and a mobile app kept citizens constantly updated with the evolving situation.

Louis Gerstner, who took the helm at IBM when the company was on the brink of a collapse, described the kind of short-term thinking needed in a major crisis in his book *Who Says Elephants Can't Dance?*: 'The last thing IBM needs right now is a vision. The real issue is going out and making things happen every day.'

However, this short-term action orientation must be balanced with a broad, holistic view of the situation and early steps to prepare the organization for what will come next.

As McKinsey consultants D'Auria and De Smet have recently noted, '[W]hat leaders need during a crisis is…mindsets that will prevent them from overreacting to yesterday's developments and help them look ahead.'[1]

---

[1] Gemma D'Auria and Aaron De Smet, 'Leadership in a Crisis: Responding to the Coronavirus Outbreak and Future Challenges,' McKinsey & Company, 2020, p. 2.

3

URBAN COMPANY (AKA URBANCLAP)

Founded in November 2014 by Abhiraj Bhal, Varun Khaitan and Raghav Chandra, Urban Company (formerly UrbanClap) is the largest home services platform in Asia, with presence in the UAE, Singapore and Australia. The company's vision is to empower millions of professionals worldwide to deliver services at home. The company offers services such as beauty and spa, cleaning, plumbing, carpentry, appliance repair, painting and more through their mobile app and website. It operates in 18 cities in India (including Ahmedabad, Bengaluru, Bhubaneswar, Chandigarh, Chennai, Delhi NCR [National Capital Region], Hyderabad, Indore, Jaipur, Kolkata, Lucknow, Ludhiana, Mumbai, Nagpur, Pune, Surat, Vadodara and Visakhapatnam) and four international markets (Dubai, Abu Dhabi, Sydney and Singapore). With a vision to organize the services ecosystem and build a community of skilled professionals, Urban Company today is home to more than 30,000 trained professionals. The company provides these micro-entrepreneurs with training, financing, insurance and product or consumables support. Urban Company is committed to creating 1 million+ micro-entrepreneurs over the next five years. To bring the whole experience together for consumers, the company invests heavily in product quality and technology. It controls its consumables supply chain and has partnered with leading brands such as L'OrMEal, Rica, O3+, Colorbar, The Man Company and Bayer. This ensures customers receive 100 per cent genuine products.

∽

We are at our best when creating enduring relationships and personal connections. When we are fully engaged, we connect with, laugh with, and uplift the lives of our employees and customers, even if it is just for a few moments. It's really about human connection.

—Howard Schultz

It is 40 degree Celsius in Delhi. All of a sudden, the air conditioner at our home stops working. My parents are sweating. The lockdown meant no availability of an AC repair service. Of course, I can informally reach out to the electrician who stays around the corner. But I am not sure how many other homes he would have informally visited, or for that matter, how he is keeping himself safe. I am not going to compromise on safety and hygiene. The AC repair has to wait till the lockdown ends and I can avail professional services.

Being stuck at home meant that we needed more of such support systems. There were more appliance breakages than ever. At the same time, hygiene of the service provider and safety protocols trump everything else. On 18 May, when Urban Company reopened their services, I was one of their first customers. And it was on this day that I decided to reach out to Abhiraj Singh, one of the co-founders, with a request to feature him in my book. I was not sure if, amidst all the business planning, Abhiraj would have the time to talk to me—more so, since services were resuming after a two-month lockdown. I was humbled when Abhiraj responded and agreed for the interview. Less than a week later, I interviewed him over a video call.

The first thing that strikes me is that Abhiraj is in his office.

'We opened our office last week and approximately 5 per cent of our staff is coming to work every day on a voluntary basis,' he tells me.

While on a video call, Abhiraj is wearing a mask. Even his profile pictures across all the social media platforms have him in mask. In fact, not only has the mask been ingrained into the company's values and protocols, the company even changed its logo on 25 April. Abhiraj tells me why this was important for a company like theirs: 'Urban Company offers high-touch services. It is imperative for us to think about the safety of our customers as well as our service partners and keep that above all the economics of the business. Through our logo and brand communications, we want to reinforce the message that safety is definitely our top priority.'

Abhiraj tells me how on 8 March, he came across an article on LinkedIn: 'A friend of mine asked me to spare 30 minutes of my time in the day and read this article that talked about why business leaders needed to act now. We had been preparing ourselves gradually for the work-from-home scenario. But this article was an eye-opener and explained how one day's delay in social distancing went a long way in the number of eventual cases. Within 24 hours, we ensured all our 1,300+ employees had laptops and were set up to work from home. We immediately provided free masks and sanitizers to our service partners, instituted hygiene protocols, such as hand-washing and purchased health and income insurance for all 27,000+ of them.'

Over the next two days, Abhiraj researched about COVID-19 and realized that this was going to be a long haul. He sent a note to his core team, not mincing words about the impact and preparing them to brace the storm. He focused their energies on employee and partner safety and motivation, cash conservation and hiring. On 14 March, he communicated to his board the key focus areas.

'Within a couple of days, my timeline of this pandemic changed from weeks to months to quarters,' he tells me.

A few days earlier, the company was busy preparing for a busy summer season, ramping up their technician training and standard operating procedures (SOPs) on installing ACs, air coolers and refrigerators. A few days later, the company's leadership was back to the drawing board, carving out a plan focused on health, safety and well-being of employees and service partners—a plan they called 'Mission Shakti' ('shakti' being the Hindi word for 'power').

The mission had three pillars: Kavach (making services safe), Vishwas (supporting the service partners) and Josh (safety and well-being of the employees).

As part of Project Kavach, Urban Company rolled out protocols around daily temperature checks; provided more than a million masks, gloves, goggles and sanitizers to the service partners. Partners were trained in the World Health Organization (WHO)-prescribed standards on using single-use sachets and sanitizing tools after every use. Services such as repair and cleaning were made completely contactless.

Abhiraj tells me about one of the many ways in which they acted responsibly. 'We were the first company to roll out a paid sick leave programme for our service partners, who were asked not to worry about salary cuts or job security. They were asked to stay at home if they showed the slightest symptom.'

At a time when most other small and medium businesses (SMBs) were laying off their staff, Urban Company was hiring and expanding to newer verticals. The company started newer categories such as sanitization and disinfection for business-to-business (B2B) space. They also opened a new category for weekly cleaning of homes, in the absence of the regular maids. They also opened up new categories for online engagement of kids and several online skill-development services. All this needed onboarding of new service partners to provide these services.

One of the things that the pandemic and the lockdown taught us even as individuals was the importance of adaptability. Companies too have realized the importance of agility. As Abhiraj rightly puts it: 'As a company, we cannot be wedded to one way of operating. We need to be nimble, agile and think out of the box. There was both an amplification of demand for home services, as people were at home, as well as availability of supply because partners were being laid off. All it needed was for us to bridge this gap. Unlike other companies, we work with individuals, who have expenses to procure tools and kits for their work. We approved interest-free business advances of ₹5,000 each for 22,000 service partners, amounting to a total corpus of ₹11 crore. We have already given advances worth ₹8.5 crore till mid-April and plan to disburse more in the time to come. These are zero per cent interest business advances with a delayed moratorium period.'

To assure the service partners as they go on the front line

to deliver services, the company provided them a specific health insurance and income protection plan, in addition to the existing life, accidental and health insurances. These insurances have been provided for as far as July 2021. The company set up a relief fund to support partners who get impacted medically or financially. They also reimbursed prepaid credits worth ₹2 crore.

While talking to Abhiraj, I found that Urban Company had taken some thoughtful steps to ensure employees' safety, although like many businesses, they, too, would have been grappling with concerns over revenues: 'We have partnered with Pristyn Care, a reputed Gurgaon-based healthcare platform. Through this partnership, we will offer free telemedicine consultations to our service partners and help with COVID-19 testing wherever needed. There are three ways in which we identify a service partner for doctor consultation. Either the service partner self-reports herself as sick, or their body temperature is above 99-degree Fahrenheit in the daily check-ups, or their Aarogya Setu app status shows "at risk" or "unwell". Thereafter, a free doctor consultation is facilitated by one of Pristyn Care's super specialist doctors, trained in COVID-19 assessments. If advised by the doctor, the service partner is tested for COVID-19 through Pristyn Care's network of 50 plus Indian Council of Medical Research (ICMR)-approved partnered labs across 20 cities. These tests are mostly done through home collection of samples by trained phlebotomists in PPE kits. Till the test results are declared, partners are required to self-quarantine and can avail benefits of Urban Company's paid sick leave programme. In case the test result is positive, the COVID-19 health insurance and income protection plan comes into effect.'

Throughout FY2021, the company expects to spend ₹20 crore just on protective equipment supplies to its partners. Such measures not only assure the service partners but also help reduce the stigma around COVID-19. The efforts of the company have been appreciated by top leaders as well as several state governments. If there is one phrase that describes Urban Company's core values, it is *compassionate capitalism*.

Talking about employee well-being, the core team has been conducting regular town halls and open sessions. Not only that, Urban Company has honoured all its hiring commitments. As Abhiraj tells me, 'Close to 130 full-time employees have joined us in this period. At the time our services were shut, we drove a lot of internal learning and development. Employees stepped up to teach each other. We are keeping a pulse on employee morale and doing our best to keep them motivated.'

Even though the company's FY2021 projections have been thrown out of the window, Abhiraj is not perturbed. 'When times like these hit, the bottom lines are trivial in the larger scheme of things. We started the year with a strong balance sheet, and were fortunate with two rounds of fundraising last year. This is a marathon and we will not try to sprint. The otherwise unorganized market that had a disproportionate share will now get more organized for good. The "cheese has moved", as they say.'

Reopening the business after the lockdown was not easy either. There were zones which were green one day and red the next. The company tuned its technical infrastructure to dynamically configure areas such that the orders were taken from and service partners assigned from only the green zones. The business for home appliance installation and repair, disinfecting and sanitizing picked up. Beauty is gaining traction.

'The government is doing its bit in balancing lives vs livelihood. The onus is now on companies like us to take measures to contain the spread of the virus. I don't think we live in a zero-risk world any more. There is nothing post-COVID. It is with COVID. The recovery is going to be slow and we need to be patient. As customers see our commitment to their safety and convenience, we expect them to come to us. As Winston Churchill once said, "This is not the end. It is not even the beginning of the end. But it is, perhaps, the end of the beginning."'

Abhiraj believes that the migrants are unlikely to come back to the metros. He believes and has been an advocate of a national labour registry programme that allows a mapping of gig workers to the availability of work in their vicinity. 'The absence of a social security layer has hit a large part of the country. Urban Company is partnering with other aggregators and the government to accelerate a social security programme for the country's unorganized labour force,' he shares with me.

Besides helping their immediate employees, customers and service partners, Abhiraj has partnered with several industry leaders to form a ₹100 crore grant fund under the umbrella of Action COVID-19 Team (Act) grants. The initiative seeks to fund capital-efficient, scalable solutions from NGOs and innovative start-ups whose solutions are a force multiplier in the battle against COVID. The initiative has received close to 1,200 applications and has funded 36 start-ups so far. The solutions span across quarantine management, contact tracing, telemedicine, medical equipment, testing kits, mental health, etc. The list of donors includes Bill & Melinda Gates Foundation, Michael & Susan Dell Foundation and Wadhwani Foundation.

'I have been spending 30–40 per cent of my time on this initiative, studying the various applications and working with the industry in closely mentoring the start-ups that can have an impact on the society's war against the pandemic. The grantee companies have helped India double its testing capabilities. Fifty per cent of the testing kits have come from one of these grantees. Ethereal Machines, one of the grantees, has designed a splitter uniquely designed for managing two patients with different ventilator needs (differential pressure splitting), while also preventing cross-contamination between paired patients. We are working with state governments in deploying these solutions at scale,' shares Abhiraj.

One would assume that in all of this, Abhiraj would have no time for himself. But what Abhiraj tells me next brings a smile to my face: 'We had a baby girl in December. The silver lining in all of this is that it is allowing me to take care of my life and spend time with my baby.

'As an entrepreneur, I was like a pendulum. Every rise and fall would keep me anxious.

But events like these reaffirmed the belief that in life, contrary to what we feel, we don't control much. We need to let go. Focus on what one can do and not worry about the rest. Such black swan events are humbling, despite our best efforts. On a spiritual side, one needs to go within and not be impacted by what is external. Troughs and peaks are two sides of the same coin and need to be embraced by the same level of detachment. Nothing is forever. Never say never.'

As I end our conversation, I am in awe of this leader who is taking care of his people, while being focused on the long term, being nimble and adaptable and yet seeing everything as an observer.

About Abhiraj Bhal

Abhiraj Bhal, co-founder of Urban Company, spent his formative years majorly in Mumbai, where he did his schooling from Navy Children's School. He holds a bachelor's degree in Electrical Engineering from the Indian Institute of Technology (IIT) Kanpur, where he was on the Dean's list, and a master's in Business Administration from the Indian Institute of Management (IIM) Ahmedabad, where he was an industrial scholar. He enjoys playing tennis and squash and has always had a keen interest in adventure sports, such as skydiving.

Abhiraj is responsible for operations and service provider onboarding at UrbanClap. Prior to UrbanClap, he was a consultant with The Boston Consulting Group, advising Fortune 500 companies across India, Germany and South-east Asia.

Abhiraj has won numerous awards, such as the Fortune 40 Under 40 (2017) and The Forbes 30 Under 30 (2017). Most recently, he won The Entrepreneur Award at NTLF2020 Global Leadership Awards. He is on the NASSCOM Internet Council and the Domestic Workers Sector Skill Council of the Government of India.

4

ZERODHA

Zerodha is a bootstrapped company which has pioneered the concept of discount broking in India. It kick-started operations on 15 August 2010 with the goal of breaking barriers that traders and investors face in India in terms of cost, support and technology. Today, their disruptive pricing models and in-house technology have made them the largest Indian stock broker by active retail clients, and the biggest by trading volumes on the top Indian stock exchanges. Zerodha was adjudged Economic Times Startup of the Year in 2020.

Coin is India's first direct mutual fund and equity platform that lets customers buy mutual funds online, completely commission-free, directly from asset management companies. In line with its philosophy, Coin is available free of any brokerage. It has a total of ₹4,500 crore assets under management (AUM). KITE is India's first multilingual trading platform available in 10 different Indian languages. Over one million clients place several million orders every day through Zerodha's powerful ecosystem of investment platforms, contributing to over 12–15 per cent of all Indian retail volumes.

In addition, it runs a number of popular, free-for-all open online educational and community initiatives (including Zerodha Varsity) to empower retail traders and investors. Rainmatter, the company's fintech fund and incubator, has invested in several fintech start-ups with the goal of growing the Indian capital markets.

∽

The fundamental law of investing is the uncertainty of the future.

—Peter Bernstein

Two years ago, a friend of mine, Nistha Tripathi, came out with a book *No Shortcuts*, which is the author's journey with the founders of 15 start-ups, who rose from humble beginnings to create a niche for themselves in the Indian start-up universe. The story that stood out for me was the story of Nithin Kamath, the founder of Zerodha. Two years later, when I decided to reach out to Nithin for my book, Zerodha was no longer a start-up. It is now the largest brokerage in India. With over 20 lakh customers, close to half of whom are active every day on the platform, Zerodha holds over 15 per cent of all retail daily order volumes in India.

In a year when companies found it hard to survive, Zerodha has been adjudged the Economic Times Start-up of the Year Award, 2020.[1] There was no better time than this crisis to prove its leadership mettle. Competing against the likes of BYJU's, bigbasket and Postman, what stood out for the jury was the resilience of the business run by Zerodha, defying all models and conventional wisdom.

I looked up Nithin's contact information and wrote him an email soliciting his time for an interview. I got a prompt revert in the next few hours. The same day, he connected me to a few members of his core team to take it ahead. We got talking. Despite his willingness to do the interview, Nithin found it hard to find time. And that was expected. Amidst a 100 per cent growth in new accounts month-on-month since the pandemic, the volatility in the market and leading his employees out of the crisis, Nithin had a lot on his plate. We were finally able to find a time to meet. But as luck would have it, the day before our first conversation, the prime minister announced the largest relief measures of ₹20 lakh crore for the country. It was the day when Zerodha witnessed its highest-ever single day trading. A few of Zerodha's customers encountered technical glitches and took to social media, blasting them for not being reliable. Nithin

---

[1] https://economictimes.indiatimes.com/small-biz/startups/newsbuzz/et-startup-awards-2020-brokerage-firm-zerodha-selected-startup-of-the-year/articleshow/77711970.cms, last accessed on 2 December 2020.

got into discussions with his technology and PR counterparts in leading the company out of this situation and scaling for the future. The company's response clarified the situation:

> We had the highest number of concurrent users today and processed the largest number of orders ever. There was absolutely no downtime except for two extremely small hiccups that affected a very small portion of our users. Between 9:15 to 9:18, we had intermittent leased line re-connections with NSE at our data centre B. This new data centre went live last week, and the orders from a small segment of users pass through the new leased lines there. Orders flowing through this particular line were slow or rejected for the first few minutes and it got resolved immediately on its own.[1]

I was finally able to meet Nithin a few days later.

In a time when everyone else was talking about unemployment, job losses, salary cuts, deaths due to the pandemic and more deaths due to starvation and apathy, it was ironic that some of us also had enough time to trade in the market. Nithin tells me why the trade was seeing an uptick. 'We have seen a massive appetite for trading, especially as people have been working from home and have free time at hand. The international market volatility in January gave us an early glimpse of what was to hit the Indian markets. We realized this was coming to India soon and started preparing for the scale. Since then, volatility has kept people active, as they are eager to make the best use of this time to invest and make money.'

In January 2020, Zerodha's chief technology officer (CTO), Kailash Nadh, observed the patterns in the market. He was quick to see that this needed scaling. The core team expedited the launch of their new data centre in order to be prepared. In parallel, news of lockdown in various parts of the world prompted Nithin to start

---

[1]https://zerodha.com/z-connect/tradezerodha/we-were-not-down-today, last accessed on 2 December 2020.

experimenting with work from home. He knew that employee safety was critical and needed to be put on the forefront of their strategy of dealing with the crisis.

'I have always been a work-from-office person. I just could not fathom how an entire company could work from home. But this time, it was not a choice, but the need of the hour. So, I kept my mental picture aside and the team got running on the ground.'

12 March onwards, Zerodha's employees started working from home.

As the market volatility increased, the trading and customer acquisition numbers flew through the roof. When traditional brokerage firms that opened the accounts offline and through physical touchpoints suddenly could not reach their customers to complete the processes, Zerodha's online processes gave it an advantage. The month-on-month numbers grew 100 per cent.

Nithin tells me how, traditionally, the offline brokerage firms held the bulk of the trade. They allowed people to trade first and give money later. Firms accepted cheques instead of digital money. But the crisis exposed the need to completely digitize. 'And that change is for good,' he says.

He also tells me how traditional firms have let people decide completely for themselves, even without making them aware of the associated risks. Automated and artificial intelligence-based solutions are now being provided and customers are moving towards leveraging technology to make data-backed trading decisions.

'The volatility will continue through the crisis. With interest rates going down and real estate in limbo, more money is expected to flow into the market. Every few days, all our previous daily records are broken; be it in terms of new customers or daily trades. We were lucky that we were working on a new data centre and could scale. We also realized that a lot of what we do currently can be replaced by automation. There is a need to reskill most of the team to ensure they don't become redundant.'

Zerodha has also been working to ensure the safety of its

customers during this time. The company knows that the entire situation is making its traders, especially new traders, more gullible to fraud and scamsters.

'We have always wanted to avoid situations where people can get conned on our platform. The Securities and Exchange Board of India (SEBI) is also doing its bit in this. The Karvy mega scam a year ago has led to SEBI working on a few regulatory changes that compromise on traders' safety. The regulation announcement has been slightly delayed by the current situation. But we are hopeful they will roll out soon. We have blocked new purchases in illiquid penny stocks, option contracts and called on other firms to also do the same.'

Features such as putting a small tag of 'event' next to a stock have started indicating a significant upcoming milestone for that company, be it declaration of results or dividends,. Unlike earlier, one can now place long-standing target and stop loss orders for Nifty and Bank Nifty futures and options positions on Zerodha's portal. The other growth engine, which is expected to kick off soon, is lending. Zerodha obtained a non-banking financial company (NBFC) licence in 2019 so it can issue loans against securities. These are typically one-year loans of about ₹50,000, with an interest rate of 12–15 per cent. Loans against securities are usually the forte of banks, and something primarily reserved for high net worth individuals. Zerodha intends to change this.

'We don't see many loans being given to retail individuals in this route because for banks, the interest rate they make on personal loans is higher,' says Nithin.

As Nithin tells me his story, I can partly relate to it. I was a Paytm employee when demonetization happened and it brought in the same opportunities and challenges that Zerodha is going through now. It is imperative to not just scale up the systems but also keep employees motivated amidst all the social media escalations for systems not working. Added to it, employees are working from home. And that brings with it a whole new set of opportunities as well as challenges.

It needs a team to come out of such a crisis and Zerodha has that.

The whole COVID situation has provided a lens to leaders who are now considering work from home as a permanent system, whereby a set of employees can alternate and work from home. This can help cut costs not just for the company but has a lot of other benefits too.

'This entire situation has stress tested our biases against work-from-home. Three hundred people from my team are right now working from their homes in Tier-II cities. Some of them are even in their villages. Imagine a system where they can work from their homes even after the crisis is over. Not only will it decongest our cities, which were never meant to handle this massive population overload, it will also help our Tier-II cities and villages to grow. These employees will be able to save a lot more, for the same salaries,' says Nithin, who till a few months ago had always only worked from office.

And believe me, Zerodha is not the only organization thinking on these lines. I have been in touch with several industry leaders and they seem to be thinking alike. Here is an opportunity in this crisis, an opportunity that can change our lifestyles forever. Who knows, traffic jams may be a thing of the past!

Nithin keeps his staff engaged via virtual conversations, fun events and video meetings. He does talk about the cons of working from home.

'Even though productivity from home is stabilizing, people are missing the workplace. People love to meet people and have a human connection. They are getting burnt out sitting at home. There is no substitute for a face-to-face meeting. When a few people could have a watercooler conversation, now all of that is happening on Zoom calls and chats. There is constant chatter and noise around at home. It is quite distracting. If the situation continues, mental well-being of people is likely to become a major health problem.'

At a personal level too, Nithin is finding it hard to disconnect. 'Personally for me, I am working much longer than when I was at office. I am sleeping less. I am constantly thinking about work and unable to disconnect. I did not have a separate workstation at home. My favourite spot to work in the house has always been the dining table. But in the first week of WFH, I added over three kg, snacking the whole day. So, I have now moved to a spot on the terrace. It is a tall table, and I think standing up while working is much healthier. But the bull run continues even on the weight front.'

Despite all the crazy demands of work life and the unusual everyday events that keep Nithin occupied, he is working with his brother, Nikhil Kamath, co-founder of Zerodha, to help the poor and homeless people. In this battle against the pandemic, they have pledged ₹25 crore for various initiatives. This includes funds to the various relief funds, including those providing medical equipment for healthcare workers, supplying meals and ration to the poor, as well as the Action COVID-19 Team (ACT) fund set up by the Government of India. Zerodha is also actively investing in start-ups focussed on climate change.

As we speak, the Zerodha founders are supplying close to 15,000 meals a day via the Bengaluru police.

'The demand for food is huge. If you go into one of these slums with, say, 5,000 packets of food, there are 15,000 people who are hungry and in need of it. What we are doing is probably not even enough for 1 percent of the people in need,' Nithin says.

On the business front, does Nithin expect the bull run to continue?

'In the short term, the business is going to grow. Even in the 2008 financial crisis, that year was indeed a great year when measured in terms of the volume of transactions. But towards late 2009, the realization set in and people noticed wealth being destroyed. The period of 2010–12 saw recession for the trading firms. So, a downturn is around the corner.

'But, unlike 2008, the downturn is not expected to be long. As long as businesses have strong fundamentals and 90 per cent of the industries survive, intelligent investing will yield good dividends.'

Unusual events such as crude oil futures dropping to negative levels make things interesting. Reduced trading timings did not allow brokerage firms to react to such a big move in the international markets. As a result, commodity brokerage firms faced huge potential losses.

'These black swan events can definitely pose a significant risk to Indian markets,' Nithin says.

In the end, I ask a question that almost everyone who interviews him would be asking: What are some investment tips for me?

'It is important to be cautious and ensure adequate liquidity for contingencies. I recommend holding a liquid component of at least 25 per cent at individual portfolio levels. The key remains to enter the markets in a measured, systematic manner without leverage and with ample diversification,' Nithin advises me.

Zerodha's story is fascinating in many ways—a start-up, a pandemic, an opportunity and the challenges. Zerodha continues to focus on people, be it employees or customers and doing the right thing for the society.

About Nithin Kamath

Nithin Kamath is the co-founder and chief executive officer (CEO) of Zerodha. The winner of 'EY Entrepreneur of the Year 2017 Start-up', Nithin has been an avid trader in the Indian capital markets for over a decade. He, along with his brother Nikhil, founded Zerodha in 2010. In addition, Nithin has been working on creating an ecosystem for spurring innovation in the financial technology industry in India. He has founded Rainmatter, an R&D fintech incubator and fund that has invested in several fintech start-ups. He also launched a 'Broking as a service' platform, where Zerodha's entire brokerage and its technology platforms are available on the cloud for developers and start-ups to build their own platforms, the first of its kind in the world. Nithin recently got featured as a successful entrepreneur in Forbes India's 'Tycoons of Tomorrow' list for 2018, along with Nikhil. He featured in the prestigious ET 40 Under 40, 2018. In

2014, he won the Confederation of Indian Industries (CII) 'Emerging Entrepreneur of the Year' award. In its annual business review, the *Economic Times* featured Kamath as one of the 10 Indian businessmen to watch out for. Zerodha has also won the 'ET Startup Award of the Year (Bootstrap) 2016' and, most recently, Nithin was adjudged one of the achievers in the finance sector at BW 40 under 40 in 2017. Outside of work, Nithin enjoys spending time with his family, playing the guitar, poker, running, playing football and basketball, and swimming.

LESSON 2
THINKING CUSTOMER BACKWARDS

Sometime in April, a restaurant sent me a message on how they had just launched a new dish and wanted me to come and try the same. Around the same time, I also received a message from another restaurant about the safety protocols they would be following as I walk in. Who do you think I would have visited? No brainer, right?

During the crisis, I struggled with trying to get refunds for services not delivered. Granted the company might have been facing its own set of internal issues, but I should have got some proactive communication with a broad sense of time frame by when my concern would get resolved.

A few companies, however, just seemed to be launching the right set of products I needed. From being able to avail at-home beautician services with her wearing extensive protective gear to requesting for a complete sanitization of the cab before it came to pick me after dropping the previous passenger, even if these came at incremental cost, were just the right steps taken by businesses that helped me become confident about availing their services. Similarly, Milkbasket started charging for ₹3–7 extra per delivery, but they shortened the ordering window for the next day, and all of this was explained to me in their app. All these were great examples of thinking customers backwards.

ITC prioritized production of essential goods, launched newer hygiene products at breakneck speeds. Designermasks got together a team of 3,000 artisans to produce customized designer masks. The Shapoorji Pallonji group invested in augmented reality solutions for selling their residential units. Google Maps invested in solutions to help merchants during the times of crisis. ACT FiberNet did not expand to newer customers but rather focused on delivering reliable internet to existing customers.

Of course, each of these companies had a pre-planned roadmap, a set of features their engineering team would be interested in building; a few easy wins and opportunities to grow the market. It was tempting to continue solving the old problems and building over existing solutions. But in a crisis, one needs to make fewer mistakes in the choice of the problem and have a focussed approach towards picking solutions.

For a few of these companies, the crisis may even mean they could sell something at a higher cost to their customers. But leadership is about none of that. Leadership is rather customer backwards. Leadership is more purpose-driven and about how one can help the customers and the community, than make some quick bucks. Leaders I spoke to believed that quick money was not worth the customer's trust. During the COVID-19 pandemic, companies that lead with empathy and genuinely address customer needs can strengthen relationships.

Leaders in my book demonstrate the customer backwards thinking in many ways: being accessible to one's customers; prioritizing among them, if needed, so that the ones in distress and with more urgent needs can be addressed first; introducing more do-it-yourself ways for customers to solve their issues; ensuring safety of the customers when delivering the service; not using this an opportunity to make additional revenue; adapting one's product line to enable the customers to respond to the crisis at their own personal levels; and making human and emotional connects than just a transactional one.

5

DELHI POLICE

Founded in 1861, Delhi Police is the law-enforcement agency for the National Capital Territory of Delhi (NCT) and is one of the largest metropolitan police forces in the world, employing close to 80,000 police personnel. About 25 per cent of its total strength is earmarked for VVIP security. Delhi Police comes under the jurisdiction of the Ministry of Home Affairs (MHA), Government of India. Considering Delhi is the capital of India and is the centre of a wide range of political, cultural, social and economic activities, Delhi Police has to play a critical role in the maintenance of law and order; including VVIP security, crime control and investigation, traffic management, etc. It is considered to have the most advanced administrative system in India.

Delhi Police has 15 Police Districts with 178 'territorial' police stations and five specialized crime units declared as Police Stations namely, Economic Offence Wing, Crime Branch, Special Cell, Special Police Unit for Women and Children (SPUWAC) and Vigilance.

Since the pandemic, over 2,000 challans[1] have been issued by the Delhi Police for violation of COVID norms.

∽

The challenge of leadership is to be strong, but not rude; be kind, but not weak; be bold, but not bully; be thoughtful, but not lazy; be humble, but not timid; be proud, but not arrogant; have humour, but without folly.

—Jim Rohn

---

[1] An official form or document, such as a receipt, invoice or summons.

Prior to the COVID-19 pandemic, my image of a police officer was one of someone who fights criminals, conducts raids and encounters and is often detached from the people they are entrusted to look after. My limited encounter with the force was at best for petty crimes such as cell phone theft. But when the pandemic hit, the force was suddenly everywhere. Be it patrolling outside our homes and asking us to stay indoors or registering the migrant labourers for their journey back home, the role of police has undergone a significant change in the last few months. At a time when the national capital of the country is among the worst-hit cities, Delhi Police is building public trust in the force through its humanitarian response to COVID-19.

Eish Singhal, deputy commissioner, Delhi Police, is one of the most humble people I came across as I went about my journey of writing this book. Eish handles Lutyens' Delhi, where our president, prime minister and the who's who of the central government reside. Under the jurisdiction of his nine police stations are the Parliament Street, Supreme Court, High Court and Jantar Mantar. Clearly, it can't be an easy area to administer. As Eish puts it, 'A large part of our duties before the pandemic were around smooth movement of the political leaders across the city, especially the prime minister, president and visiting foreign ministers. The sensitivity of the area and the presence of Jantar Mantar, the focal point for all kinds of protests, always kept us on our toes.'

When the government announced the first lockdown, Delhi Police was instructed to enforce it, but locking down the district that housed Rashtrapati Bhavan, all the offices and residences of the ministries, the embassies and the judicial courts was extremely sensitive and required a lot more deliberation and planning at the highest levels.

'While the nation was locked down, the ministries across the central and state governments were functioning to ensure the supply of essential services. Overnight, we needed to issue movement authorization to over 11,000 people. We deployed pickets at several points to ensure only authorized movement. There were incidents when someone without a pass would want to move around for critical work. Each such case was dealt on a case-by-case basis and by establishing direct communication channels of the on-ground force with the highest level officers, including myself,' Eish tells me.

The police were tasked with keeping people at home.

'I first ensured my district policemen were trained in safety protocols. For example, earlier, two men would go on a bike for patrolling. Now only one would go. Same for the barricades.

'Department-wide training on how to keep citizens indoors by educating them rather than using force was given. Corrective actions and punishments were tried to be kept to minimum. During the crisis, the boundaries between the municipal corporation and the police blurred.

'Maximum crowd was seen outside grocery stores, medical clinics, chemists and hospitals. We drew circles demarcating the areas where people could stand. We kept guard when the crowd seemed to get restless. Few of our staff, especially the ones assigned hospital duties, were given personal protective equipment (PPE) kits for their safety. We also worked to create a team of citizens who volunteered to help us in our initiatives. These volunteers were trained to educate people in their localities about the safety protocols and they became our extended arms and were in constant touch with my team to communicate the ground situation.'

Eish's jurisdiction employs 2,000 policemen, many of whom have come from across other states to work. As the state borders were sealed, senior officers across the districts worked with the officers and officials from Uttar Pradesh and Haryana to ensure that their officers could come for duty, without any issues.

'We were learning from what was happening on ground, communicating those issues to our seniors, brainstorming with them and implementing suggestions in easing the situation. For example, when a few officers expressed concerns about their family's safety if they went home every day after having interacted with so many people, we decided to work with local authorities. The New Delhi Municipal Council (NDMC) gave us a few marriage halls where our officers could stay free of cost. At the same time, prolonged periods of being away from family were causing them grief. So we worked out a schedule such that part of the force could go home on a rotational basis.'

Although the government called for contractors and business owners to continue to pay salaries to their staff, businesses shut down and people were left without a job or shelter. Migrant unrest began to grow and social distancing norms began to be flouted. The police were tasked with maintaining law and order and social distancing at key focal points of aggregation, ranging from travel registration centres for their immigration to their hometowns to railway stations.

'We worked with the government and municipal bodies to move as many people as possible to the shelter homes. On one hand, the huge flux of the migrants was a chaos and on the other, the mental and physical well-being of our staff was of utmost importance. Men, women and children were battling the 40 degree summer and jostling to take the next train or bus possible. It was a challenge for the police to explain the significance of social distancing to those who feared for their livelihood,' Eish tells me.

The district houses two of the most prominent hospitals of Delhi, the Ram Manohar Lohia Hospital as well as Lady Hardinge Medical College, both of which were also dedicated COVID treatment centres. Stray incidents of health workers being abused came to our notice. The police was deployed round the clock to ensure the safety of front-line workers.

'The stigma around COVID led to people trying to escape the isolation centres. It is hard on patients, especially when they are isolated and when the patient next to them becomes severely ill and in some cases, passes away. The mental stress and trauma of isolation leads the sanest person to behave in the weirdest of ways. Officers posted in these hospitals often felt the pain and suffering and were impacted by it. Those who formed the part of the post-mortem unit suffered mental trauma. It was important to keep rotating the staff, so that no one was on such stressful duties for long.'

Home isolation was the most difficult to ensure. People went to the extent of tearing the quarantine notices stuck outside their homes. When healthcare workers went to people's homes, they were ill-treated and asked to leave. Contact tracing also needed coercion. When containment zones were announced, the police were given the duty of sealing the areas.

The role of the police was in ensuring the enforcement of the lockdown and quarantine measures along with the other teams on the front line. In all of this, they had to ensure that the crime rate was kept low. As people stayed inside, domestic violence and cybercrimes became growing concerns.

On one hand, the police played the role of enforcement and were sometimes seen as stern and ruthless; on the other hand, several policemen worked in their individual capacities as well as in groups to help people. When individuals and non-governmental organizations (NGOs) approached the police asking how they could help, the police knew which areas were most severely affected and started working with these NGOs and individuals. One such area was distribution of food to the needy. Many officers contributed in their capacities towards these causes.

'The Delhi Sikh Gurdwara Management Committee has been providing over 75,000 meals daily to the needy. In order to motivate them and keep their spirits up, I worked with my staff to do a "parikrama" of the Bangla Sahib Gurudwara. A total of five police cars, nine gypsies and 30 patrol bikes paid tribute to the noble act. This event motivated not just the gurudwara but also our own staff, as they built a human connection with these good Samaritans. One of our sub-inspectors donated masks made by his mother.'

Above and beyond their duties, the police have been lending a helping hand to the senior citizens in their district. Whether it is about supplying essentials to their doorstep or about celebrating their birthdays, whether it is about getting a loved one to meet them or tele-consultation, Eish is proud of how his team is lending a healing touch.

'We started getting a lot of calls from senior citizens and some of them just wanted to see another human being around them. More than a professional duty, this was our duty towards humanity. A station house officer (SHO), South Avenue composed ghazal, motivating people to fight against the pandemic. Another sub-inspector made two motivational videos to keep the whole atmosphere joyous.'

The pandemic also showed its ugly sides when people abandoned their deceased family members due to fear of getting infected.

'A task, often unattended, needed the most experienced officers, who had to follow the guidelines while honourably cremating the abandoned bodies.'

Amidst all the work, the safety and well-being of the officers were top of the list for Eish. Regular sanitization of the police stations, police vehicles, pickets and barracks was also carried out. Special cells were set up just outside the station entrance to ensure not many people flocked the station and the risk was minimized.

'We have been conducting regular yoga camps and distributing nutrition supplements to our staff. Despite our best efforts, a few of the police officers got infected. We have been constantly engaging with our staff and reiterating the importance of wearing masks and protective gears, especially as the lockdown opens up.'

A few police officers have unfortunately succumbed to the pandemic. Like any other organization, the police department planned a few things in advance, and adapted and reacted to many others as they came along. Like other organizations, the department is doing the balancing act of keeping the system running while also ensuring their own staff is safe and well. And it is touching lives in ways more than one could imagine. From being #DilliKiPolice (police of Delhi) to #DilKiPolice (police of heart). And leaders such as Eish are on the forefront of this transformation.

About Eish Singhal

IPS Officer Dr Eish Singhal is the Deputy Commissioner of Police, New Delhi district. He has been with the police force since 2012. During these years, he has worked across traffic police as well as law-and-order management. Eish has received several awards and letters of appreciation for his work in ensuring traffic management and law and order during several important events. Some of the most recent appreciations have come from the Embassy of the United States (US), New Delhi for support during the visit of the US president, Donald Trump, on 24 and 25 February 2020 at New Delhi as well as from the Embassy of Israel, New Delhi for support and assistance rendered in facilitating the security arrangements for urgent and safe evacuation of Israeli tourists from India during the ongoing COVID-19 pandemic and lockdown in India. Eish loves playing lawn tennis and golf during his free time.

6

DELHI GOVERNMENT ADMINISTRATION

The District Administration of Delhi is the enforcement department for all kinds of Government of Delhi and Government of India policies and exercises supervisory over numerous other functionaries of the government.

Delhi has a total of 11 districts. Each of these districts is headed by an Indian Administrative Service (IAS) officer of the rank of Deputy Commissioner (DC). The general administration of the district is vested with the DC. He is at once the DC, district magistrate and collector. As DC, he is the executive head of the district, with multifarious responsibilities relating to development, panchayats, local bodies, civil administration, etc. As district magistrate, he is responsible for law and order and heads the police and prosecuting agency. As collector, he is the chief officer of the revenue administration and is responsible for the collection of land revenue, and is also the highest revenue judicial authority in the district. He acts as the district elections officer and the registrar for registration work and exercises overall supervision on other government agencies in his district.

DCs report to the Divisional Commissioner of Delhi (Principal Secretary of Revenue), who further reports to the Chief Secretary of Delhi. Apart from the district-level DCs, there are also DCs who coordinate work among the various local bodies, departments and agencies for proper administration.

∼

Leadership is not a position or a title, it is action and example.

—Cory Booker

We sit in our homes, discussing and debating on the government's policies and actions. When they lock us down, we criticize them for not thinking about the poor and the displaced. When they unlock, we criticize them for not prioritizing lives over livelihood. Some say they did not act fast enough, some say they acted abruptly. When cases spike, we hurl abuses at them. We all have our right to have an opinion. But who exactly is behind these decisions and their execution, besides the elected representatives. Behind all the decision-making and execution of the decisions at the nation, state, district and ward levels is not just an army of policymakers but also the unsung IAS officers, who work away from the limelight. They are responsible for providing all the data to the government to help it make appropriate decisions, as well as executing those decisions by working with thousands of stakeholders. They take the central decisions, translate them into what it means for their state and then work with the district administrations in the planning and implementation at district and ward levels. They form a feedback loop back up to the state and the central levels. They are the pulse of the common man. In this centralized planning and decentralized implementation strategy, they are a bridge between us and the highest government machinery.

Abhishek Singh is one of them. Working tirelessly since the pandemic hit the country, he has been a critical bridge between the policymakers and those who need to execute. What is unique is that Abhishek is part of the team of administrators for one of the newest state governments of the country and one that is critical at not just a state but also the national level—the Delhi government. What is special is that Delhi is my home, the place I grew up and would always remain connected to.

I am introduced to Abhishek by his wife, Durga Shakti Nagpal. Durga, too, is an IAS officer and has been working with the highest echelons of the government. The nature of her role limits her from being neutrally interviewed. When I reach out to Abhishek for an interview, he tells me about his availability. Most of my calls with him happen around midnight. During the day time, he stays busy with his work. Abhishek has lost track of days. It takes him a while to recollect what he was doing on the job before the pandemic.

'The Delhi government took oath on 16 February. We were working with the government in understanding their five-year vision and aligning our administrative charter to it,' Abhishek recalls.

Delhi was widely hit by the protests against the Citizenship Amendment Bill (CAB) at that time. And the situation refused to fade away. But for the pandemic.

'Much before the Centre's Janata curfew, the Government of Delhi proactively announced the closure of primary schools across Delhi as a precautionary measure.'

A series of shutdowns were announced and gatherings restricted. On 13 March, the government issued an order prohibiting gatherings involving more than 200 people, such as seminars, conferences and the Indian Premier League (IPL) cricket matches. This was further restricted to 50 people on 16 March, and to 20 people on 19 March when the number of cases rose to 12. Between 12 and 16 March, the government ordered the closure of cinema halls, public swimming pools, gyms and night clubs until 31 March. On 19 and 20 March, sports complexes and shopping malls were also ordered to be shut down. All restaurants were ordered to discontinue sitting arrangements until 31 March. Private establishments were ordered to allow their employees to work from home till 31 March.

On 22 March, when the number of cases rose to 29, the Delhi government announced the lockdown in the state until 31 March. The lockdown involved (i) suspending public transport services, (ii) sealing borders with Haryana and Uttar Pradesh, (iii) suspending all domestic and international flights arriving in Delhi, and (iv) putting a ban on the congregation of more than five persons at any public place. This was followed by a nationwide lockdown enforced by the central government between 25 March and 14 April, which was then extended till 3 May and then beyond.

'The administrative machinery was kicked in to work with

the various districts in execution of each of these steps. Delhi has a total of 11 districts and 272 wards. The district magistrates did a daily reporting of the state of their districts. We would identify loopholes, if any, and work with the district to plug those. The key focus was on creating social awareness about the pandemic, need for social distancing and making sure the health infrastructure was well equipped to handle the scale. I worked with districts to assess the existing hospital capacities in terms of doctors, beds, ventilators and protection equipment for the staff. The district reports were aggregated at a state level and sent to the central government, asking for help both in terms of funds and the health equipment,' Abhishek tells me.

When research established the germination period of the virus to be within 14 days, the administrative team realized they did not have enough isolation centres. Abhishek shares with me the steps taken to counter the issue.

'We worked in identifying the buildings that could potentially be used and converted to quarantine centres. Right from government buildings to hotels; right from free facilities to the more luxurious ones, we worked with the districts in the full capacity planning and monitoring set up.'

Fixed rates were negotiated with high-end hotels that were willing to convert into quarantine centres. Their staff were trained in safety protocols and asked to stay in the hotel.

'What is unique about Delhi?' I ask Abhishek.

'Many things,' he says. 'Delhi houses not just the state ministers but also the prime minister and the president of the country. Whatever happens in Delhi is covered by not just national but also international media. Delhi is diverse in its income variations, demography and religion mix. Foreign nationals come to study in Delhi University. Foreign embassies are here. Some of the top industrialists live here.

'We are also unique because major bodies such as the Indian Council of Medical Research (ICMR), major hospitals such as the All India Institute of Medical Sciences (AIIMS) are housed in Delhi. Information comes pretty fast to us.'

Just when the situation in Delhi was beginning to come under control, the Delhi faction of the Tablighi Jamaat held a religious congregational programme in Nizamuddin West. The Delhi government's order of 13 March that no seminars, conferences or any big event are to be held was apparently ignored by the organization. There were also other violations of rules by foreign speakers, including misuse of tourist visas for missionary activities and not taking 14-day home quarantine for travellers from abroad.

'The immediate priority was contact tracing and containing the spread. This needed work with the administrative machinery of several states, especially the ones where people had travelled to, after the congregation,' Abhishek tells me.

On one hand was the monster of COVID and on the other was a bigger monster of communal hatred.

Abhishek points out a finer nuance about the state of Delhi: 'Delhi is uniquely placed in the way that law and order is not a state subject.' One can understand what he means when he says, 'The administration was concerned about the spread of violence and started preparing for it with the help of the Centre.'

And just as there was a handle on this situation, the migrant labourer problem emerged. Abhishek is candid when he shares his perspective.

'We had prepared for shelters and food. Corporates, NGOs and the entire community were coming forward in helping make the arrangements. They donated generously in cash and in kind. But despite the arrangements, the social unrest was growing. No administration anticipated this.'

Was it the lack of food that led to it? Did we grossly underestimate the number of migrants? There are several questions that arise.

'We relied on the data from the employment office, ration systems, local politicians and volunteers who work on ground to understand how many migrants were we talking about. When it came to our notice that migrants did not have their ration cards, we allowed ration to be given without the cards.'

There are around 30 lakh people in Delhi who do not have ration cards. The Delhi government has provided free ration to more than 20 lakh poor people who do not have a ration card since the lockdown came into effect.

Abhishek tells me that the Delhi government didn't want to go the lockdown route. 'In the initial stages of the pandemic, the Delhi government did not want a complete lockdown, but it was the Centre's directive, which it needed to comply with. We wanted to restrict movement but not bring it to a standstill overnight. That's what happened and that led to a lot of panic,' he says.

Surveys in May lauded the Delhi chief minister as the best chief minister in dealing with the crisis. I ask Abhishek the reason for that, despite such a high infection rate. And what accounts for such a high infection rate, despite the preparedness and the efforts of the government.

'Delhi is among the most populous cities in the country. So, the spread of the virus is faster here. Delhi's testing rates are also the highest, only after Kerala. The RT-PCR test is quite difficult to conduct and needs specialized skill. Being home to the ICMR has helped with more reliable testing,' he explains.

The administration has also needed to deal with border issues, especially as the movement across the border in the NCR region has been a cause of concern for all the state governments involved.

As Delhi opens up, what does it entail for the administration?

'We are working on a continued awareness creation to keep safety in mind, while work resumes. The odd–even formula is being applied wherever possible. While the health infrastructure has been made robust, we continue to request people to display more responsible behaviour.'

Offering his personal perspectives, Abhishek wants to see more demand-driven reforms. 'If we look at what developed nations across the world are doing, we see that they are focusing on demand generation. Direct cash transfers are the need of the hour,' he says.

Does he see anything positive in the situation?

'Digitalization,' he replies. 'Our administrative work has gone online. Who would have imagined education at government schools to be completely digital? All that is happening for real and in an accelerated mode.'

Abhishek also talks about the role of the media in all of this.

'We need to be aware of the reality and prepare for it. At the very least, the media needs to help create a connected country rather than a divided one. What happens when the message that goes out is that the business owners can pay but they are not paying? They are not running charities and if they continue to pay while their businesses are shut, where will they land? We need to stop the caste, religion and region divides. We are a country of 130 crore people. Tell me one person who has not been impacted in some way or the other by the pandemic.'

I couldn't have agreed more. Radical statements damage the mindsets of people and can create civil unrest. That's what is happening at the moment and leading to a vicious cycle of panic. It is easy to criticize and judge. But people on the ground are doing their best and they are also exposed in that process.

'Despite all the digital coordination and virtual meetings, I meet at least 50 people every day. I have no clue of their being infected or of them putting me at risk. I have a five-year-old at home and an 80-year-old as well. I am scared too, but the nation needs me,' shares Abhishek. One truly feels for all the front-line workers, including those in administration, on hearing that.

Every time the Centre passes a directive or changes policy, there are immediate actions needed by the state government. Delays in execution at the ground level create confusion. Administrators are working round the clock to support the policymakers. They give inputs, opinions and data to the decision-makers. They keep an eye on the ground realities and are resolved to solve people's issues.

They are not perfect; this situation and its outcomes might not be either. But their leadership offers lessons of commitment, dedication and hard work.

About Abhishek Singh

Abhishek Singh is a 2011-batch IAS officer, under the Uttar Pradesh cadre. He underwent training in Noida and went on to join his first posting in Kanpur, where he busted a large-scale food adulteration racket. During his various postings across districts in UP and Delhi, Abhishek worked on various initiatives against land encroachment and in the education sector. Not only did he hand over an encroached land space spanning five acre to build an educational institute, he also started community initiatives to adopt a government school and strengthen both its physical infrastructure as well as the teaching capabilities by active engagement with the community.

During COVID, Abhishek has been a critical part of the Delhi administration in leading through the crisis.

Abhishek is a multi-talented individual. He started an employment initiative, SIGMA (Students for Involved Governance and Mutual Action), a one-of-a-kind, innovative, independent and voluntary 'student-run' think tank, which was started by a group of students of IIM Ahmedabad along with Abhishek and his wife. It currently has members from India's premier institutions such as IIM Bangalore, IIM Calcutta, IIT Bombay, IIT Delhi, St Stephen's College and the Tata Institute of Social Sciences, Mumbai, among others. The goal is to create a platform to leverage the fresh perspective of India's students for effective and innovative governance. SIGMA's blue-collar job initiative is lauded by several personalities and bureaucrats.

Abhishek's interests around meaningful cinema made him try his hands at acting. After a successful debut with a short film on mental health issues and being featured in a musical album, Abhishek is currently working on several web-series projects. He is also working on the concept of a one-of-its-kind talent show 'World of Worthy', which will showcase the hidden talent in our armed and uniformed forces.

LESSON 3
POWER OF COMMUNICATION

In a crisis, if there is one thing that precedes everything else, it is the power of communication.

Crisis is a time of uncertainty. The parallel unfolding of COVID-19 across the world has presented leaders with infinitely complicated challenges and no easy answers. Tough trade-offs abound, and with them, tough decisions about communicating complex issues to diverse audiences. Never have executives been put under such an intense spotlight by a sceptical public gauging the care, authenticity and purpose demonstrated by companies. Combine this with the multitudes of other external events, be it protests in the US or the India–China border tensions, people are unsure of what they don't know or what might be coming their way. This is true not just of employees, but also customers and suppliers.

You might not want newer raw material because demand is low; you might have to lay off the workforce because there is no cash; customers might need to wait for their refunds because you are prioritizing rescue operations. We are dealing with humans at the other end after all. Transparency and a path to the next steps not just helps build a relationship for the longer term but makes the other feel like a partner in that decision, rather than a recipient of the same.

For example, I was trying to contact an airline staff for a refund. And the call centre employee told me that the company was busy repatriating passengers stuck abroad. Now this employee was a leader. He demonstrated a sense of purpose, while apologizing for the short-term inconvenience this was causing to me.

Leaders I spoke to stressed on the importance of a radical candour. Regular communication sets the right expectations. Simple forums such as regular town halls rather than ad-hoc conversations help. Written messages help. Opening up the audience for questions in larger forums helps. Helping people make sense of the decisions in the context of the situation helps.

Asking for support helps. Demonstrating vulnerability helps. Sharing personal anecdotes helps. Asking for suggestions and alternate ways of doing business helps. Celebrating success helps. Accepting failures helps. Building community helps. Expressing empathy helps. Communicating without mincing words helps. Leaders also delegate more detailed communication across different functions, roles and parts of the organization and ensure the consistency of these messages and their alignment with the broader organization's communications.

Leaders need to avoid a paternalistic approach and treat stakeholders as adults who are in it together.

7
ACT

Atria Convergence Technologies (ACT) Fibernet commenced its journey as a small start-up in the video and data space in 2000, but quickly metamorphosed into India's largest non-telco and third-largest Internet Service Provider, pioneering the high-speed internet revolution in India with more than 1.5 million customers. Based out of Bengaluru, the company currently serves 19 cities across the country. ACT (Atria Convergence Technologies Ltd) was born out of a vision to become the most admired in-the-home entertainment, education and interactive services company that creates radical social transformation, and delights and empowers customers.

Symbolizing its vision, today ACT, as an organization, is close to realizing the same by representing the industry as a leader with a modest turnover of ₹1,600 crore for the fiscal 2019–20 and profitability of ₹450 crore. ACT has not just endured the ups and downs of the industry but is growing responsibly through its consistent innovations and bringing great value to its customers by partnering with over-the-top (OTT) industry giants such as Netflix, SonyLIV and ZEE5.

ACT Fibernet firmly believes that contributing towards society is one of the most pivotal responsibilities for organizations and has, thus, extended its support in bringing about transformation and being an enabler towards accomplishing the government's vision of making India a digitally powered nation. Several path-breaking initiatives have been taken up by the organization to further this vision. Aside from its pioneering presence and services across the nation, ACT has won several awards and accolades as a testament to its growing presence and excellence across the industry.

A good plan today is better than a perfect plan tomorrow.

—George S. Patton

The old phrase '*roti, kapda aur makaan*' (food, clothing and shelter), representing minimalistic lifestyle, has now been replaced with '*roti, kapda, makaan aur internet*' (food, clothing, shelter and internet). In the time of COVID, when the entire nation is in a state of lockdown and we are all staying indoors, it is impossible to imagine a world without the internet. Be it our office work, grocery shopping, classes or entertainment, everything is being done online. Reports indicate how every second Indian across various cities is using the internet every day.[1]

At my home, too, the story is no different. Throughout the day, my husband and I are on video calls/meetings with our colleagues while my parents surf the internet for news and entertainment on YouTube. In all of this, there is the presence of an organization that we do not often talk about, but this industry is the reason why we can today confidently consider work-from-home as a long-term alternative. Yes, we are talking about the broadband service providers. So, I decided to reach out to my mine, ACT, and talk to them about the interesting times this industry is witnessing.

In January 2020, Bala Malladi, the chief executive officer (CEO) of ACT, was on a vacation in the Maldives with his family. En route to home, they noticed the increased screening at the Colombo airport. Soon after they had reached home, Bala's wife sneezed a couple of times, making the family nervous.

'We realized that we were not isolated from the world. India could very well become an epicentre of infection and if that happens,

---

[1] Viveat Susan Pinto, 'Covid-19 Lockdown Effect: Every Second Indian Now on Internet in Cities,' *Business Standard*, 9 May 2020, https://www.business-standard.com/article/economy-policy/covid-19-lockdown-effect-every-second-indian-now-on-internet-in-cities-120050801805_1.html, last accessed on 3 December 2020.

the scale will be difficult to control without completely locking down the country or the infected parts of the country. Towards the latter half of February, Kerala started to report cases from people who had returned from Wuhan. Having dealt with a major business disruption in 2016, during the Chennai floods, we did not want to leave it to chance but prepare more proactively. Our network and customer base have grown since then and disruption of services at this time will not be in the best interest of our customers.'

ACT has a customer base of 1 million cable connections and 1.5 million broadband connections across 19 cities. On an average, every household has four people using broadband services. The backbone of the internet business is its data centres and manpower. And so the key areas that Bala focused on were operational continuity, information security and employee safety.

'We are one of the few companies who have not outsourced any customer touchpoint. Be it our call centres or our field staff, all of them are our full-time employees. Letting go of them was out of question. On the contrary, their safety and well-being were extremely important. The toughest decision was to balance the safety of our employees vis-à-vis delivering the service promised to our customers. We exist because of our customers and the customer base exists because of our employees.'

On one hand, the government declared the internet as an essential service and proactively asked ACT if they needed any support in ensuring connectivity to people working from home. On the other hand, the demand for new connections grew manifold, providing a lifetime business opportunity for ACT to grow its market share. However, Bala made a conscious decision to focus on the existing customers and take care of the employees.

'More than 75 per cent of our customers have been with us for more than a year. More than 50 per cent of our customers have been with us for more than three years. They needed us the most now. We could possibly expand to newer customers, but that could only happen once we had fulfilled our commitments to existing customers as well as made sure our employees were not at risk. We decided not to prioritize business acquisition and expansion at this time.'

Over the first week of March, Bala's leadership team made a 100-point tracker for the various work streams the team needed to focus on. Physical access to data centres was mission critical at all times. Each of these centres needed to be manned by at least three or four people. Even when this number was reduced to two, there still were exceptional scenarios to be handled.

'For example, in case of a power cut or failure, the generators could keep the centres running for close to 24 hours. We could increase this to 36 hours, but beyond that, someone would need to get there and refill the fuel. The situation was an unlikely scenario, a worst-case one. Nevertheless, we had to be prepared with all the permissions. We could not wait for it to happen and then struggle to respond to it. Even if the data centre was in red zones or containment zones, in this worst-case scenario, we would need physical access. We worked with government agencies for the requisite approvals,' Bala explains.

ACT had always operated as a high-touch business.

'For us, the customer's problems are *our* problems. Even when there is no issue in our network but the customer's computer has a problem, we try to address it. We debug with them and solve it for them. We have traditionally made sure one of our executives reaches the customer's home in a couple of hours, but in this situation, that is getting increasingly difficult,' Bala tells me.

ACT pivoted its operational standard operating procedures (SOPs) to remote diagnosis as much as possible and visits were made only when it was unavoidable. This helped them get two-thirds of the field staff to work remotely and only one-third of them needed to be on-ground at any point in time.

'Even in normal circumstances, our field staff goes through rigorous etiquette training. They visit a customer's homes to solve problems. During these times, they not only needed to be polite and courteous, but also ensure both their and the customers' safety. The

SOPs were changed to make their work as touchless as possible. The staff was trained on the five commandments: wearing masks, washing hands, using sanitizers, social distancing and avoiding touching the face,' Bala says.

The leadership team set up a daily morning call with the field staff, reminding them of these commandments and harping on their importance for everyone's safety. These calls also helped the leadership keep a pulse check on the staff's mental and physical well-being.

'We trained all our employees to use the workplace app. Through this, we send reminders to our staff and stay connected.'

Fibre-based networks are costly to maintain. Any minor disruption and even a millimetre cut underground can cause disruption for thousands of customers. Each such disruption is costly for the business as well as takes some time to be fixed. Special permission needs to be taken from the civil authorities to dig and go underground for repair. These works are often carried over the night to cause minimum traffic disruptions. Bala's priority was to work with the authorities and sensitize them of such possible scenarios and the support they would need, as they went about ensuring a connected nation.

'We envisaged exceptional demands on our network, both in terms of speed requirements and download capabilities. And ensured our network could step up.'

One of the other things that gave Bala sleepless nights was around information security for the customers. The call centre employees were now working from home. Sensitive information about the customers was now accessible outside the company's premises. Any leaks or callousness in handling that information was non-negotiable. The information technology (IT) team set up the appropriate virtual private network (VPN) connections with the safety and security protocols and sensitized well-meaning employees on some of these security risks and how they needed to ensure the security of the customer's data.

As Bala puts it, 'After all, they were the custodians of customer's trust and represented the ACT brand.'

Every word in our conversation speaks volumes of Bala's conviction and trust in his employees. He believes in the power of distributed leadership, empowering and trusting people. No wonder the company has been rated as an exceptional place to work by leading global organizations such as Great Place to Work.

'Happy employees create happy customers,' as Bala says. I completely agree.

Over the course of two months (March-April), government and top leaders reached out to Bala and extended their full support to retain the US$200-billion workforce, who was working from home, remotely connected. Bala requested the authorities to ensure that the field staff had the movement passes and were not blocked from moving around. Barring a few stray incidents, the team was provided full on-ground support to keep the systems running.

Confident of the robustness of their network and ability to deliver, ACT has been able to provide free upgrades to unlimited data and 300 Gbps[1] connections to more than one-third of its customers.

'We had 100 per cent additional availability of international leased line bandwidth at any given point in time. It is expensive, but it is the cost of doing business. We were sure of the promises we were making and did due diligence before being vocal about them.

'Exceptional situations demand out-of-the-box responses. We were saying no to all requests from existing customers from containment zones. We felt that it was not worth risking a life to deliver the service promise in those zones. However, several hospitals and fever clinics who needed our service contacted us. Isolated patients could suffer mental trauma if they lost connectivity with the outside world. In those situations, we equipped our staff with PPEs and asked them if they would voluntarily want to fix things. The employees stepped up and went over and above their call of

---

[1]Short for gigabits per second.

duty to provide connectivity to many such hospitals and clinics,' Bala shares with me.

Responding to a request from the Bangalore Police, the company also set up eight Wi-Fi hotspots and two TVs at a few migrant labour camps. This provided the much-needed communication and entertainment facilities for over a thousand people staying there. As we speak, the company is providing 20 Mbps[1] speed and unlimited data to the people living in those camps.

All of the company's efforts have been appreciated by its customers. ACT has been recognized as the most consistent network by several speed test surveys and industry researches. Ookla, the global leader in internet testing and analysis, recognized ACT for the highest download speeds. In a time when people troll companies on social media for the slightest of inconvenience, ACT's social media accounts receive several notes of gratitude from its customers and requests for new connections.

'These messages and notes keep the employees motivated in these tough times,' Bala says, and one can understand why.

Employee safety does keep Bala awake at night; more so now as the lockdown has opened up and touchpoints have increased. Medical advisors are constantly communicating, educating and mandating safety protocols for the field staff as they go on the front line, to deliver. The company is beginning to deliberate on calibrated new connections.

Of course, the company's corporate business has been impacted. Many small and home enterprises have shut businesses and that has made a dent on the company's (profit and loss) P&L. However, the company has not taken advantage of their individual customers or increased prices to cover for the losses.

As Bala succinctly puts it: 'It is when rubber hits the road that one needs to stand to one's convictions and core values.'

ACT has donated close to a lakh masks to the Bengaluru civic

---

[1] Short for megabits per second.

agencies to help contain the spread of the virus. Together with a sister organization, ACT is providing more than 1,50,000 meals per day. They have also provided rations to more than half a million families for more than a couple of weeks. They are working with authorities in ensuring disinfectants are not in short supply.

Bala tells me how, at a personal level, the pandemic has reaffirmed his belief that it is the greatness of the followers that make a leader. He is awed by the strength, commitment and sense of duty his team has shown in keeping their customers connected. Everyone has taken charge and led others in these trying times. By not hiking prices and seeking new customers, Bala has also sent out an important message: don't be opportunistic when someone depends on you.

As I end my discussion with Bala, I am humbled by the power of the internet. It is a thing that we all take for granted, just like the air we breathe. But it is leaders like Bala who have made it so seamless and integrated in our lives that we can afford to take it for granted; more so as our jobs depend on staying connected. Thank you, ACT!

About Bala Malladi

Bala, the CEO of ACT, is a qualified chartered accountant and has over 25 years of experience in the industry. He is a veteran of Unilever, where he has successfully completed wide-ranging projects in India and in Europe in finance, strategy and supply chain for 17 years. He also headed the commercial function of Kimberly-Clark Lever and represented Hindustan Unilever Limited (HUL) in this joint venture.

At ACT, Bala leads the blueprint of the strategic business plans, directs all business vertical heads to define their operating road map, personally oversees acquisitions under ACT and is the first in command to drive the ACT Way value system across all its operations. He has used his experience of setting up new businesses and managing large portfolios of well-known brands across the globe to establish ACT as one of the leading digital cable and broadband service providers in India. Bala is passionate about developing people and taking up small and big business initiatives of multiple dimensions.

8

TUI GROUP

TUI Group is a British-German multinational travel and tourism company headquartered in Hannover, Germany. It is the largest leisure, travel and tourism company in the world, with 1,600 travel agencies, 150 aircrafts, 16 cruise liners, 400 hotels and resorts, and presence in over 180 countries. The group owns five European airlines—the largest holiday fleet in Europe—and several Europe-based tour operators. TUI's hotel brands include several premium resorts and hotels. Its cruise lines include Hapag-Lloyd, Marella Cruises and TUI Cruises (Deutschland).

TUI India deals with four sectors of travelling, namely Special Interest Tours, Incentive Travel, Conference Management and India and International Holidays.

∼

Once a year, go someplace you've never been before.

—The Dalai Lama

Mom has travelled to Delhi and her return flight is on 28 March. I am unable to make up my mind about whether to let her fly in these times or simply cancel her flight ticket. The travel portal I booked with is ambiguous about the reschedule and cancellation policies. I try to call them, but the wait time exceeds an hour and the call keeps getting disconnected. Choice becomes involuntary when Prime Minister Narendra Modi announces the cancellation of all domestic flights starting midnight of 24 March. Many, like my mom, are stranded wherever they are.

When I think of writing this book, getting in touch with someone from the travel industry for inputs is a natural choice for me. This is primarily for two reasons: one, I have worked in the industry and understand its nuances better than the other industries I plan to research on. Two, what this industry has been going through has impacted me at a personal level with my mother not being able to return to Delhi as planned and also with our next international trip to the Maldives being cancelled. This is a sector whose revival will come long after the pandemic is over.

Travel, as an industry, has an extremely complex supply chain. Traditional tour operators and package holiday providers combine hotel and flight offerings but do not own any of these experiences. Online travel aggregators such as Yatra, MakeMyTrip, etc. work with airlines and hoteliers to provide a package to the customers. These players operate on wafer-thin margins and are driven by volumes.

Having worked in the sector, I have the advantage of knowing many senior leaders in this space. I reach out to Krishan Singh, the chief executive officer (CEO) of TUI India. Krishan has worked in the travel space for over two decades. Having worked with him directly during my stint at Yatra, I am convinced that my conversation with Krishan would be candid and insightful.

TUI is a vertically integrated business. From ownership of aircrafts, hotels and cruise liners, to several key partnerships across the world with hotel chains, excursions and activity operators as well as local transit authorities, the group covers the entire tourism value chain under one roof. This integrated offering enables 70,000 TUI staff to serve close to 27 million customers in 180 regions across the globe, but being asset-heavy comes at its own cost. During such pandemics, the company needs to not just take care of its employees and clients but also invest heavily in the maintenance of their fixed assets.

The group's presence in China brought with it some early signs of the crisis. When several regions across the globe started announcing lockdowns, the group's top priorities were to get all the ongoing tourists back to their base stations and to ensure that the on-ground staff across the globe was able to work from home and there weren't any connectivity or accessibility issues.

'There was huge pressure on the TUI India call centre employees, almost 10 times that of normal days. Panic-stricken customers wanted to cancel or postpone their upcoming travels; people were worried about their money getting stuck with us. Our domestic staff partnered with the staff around other parts of the world and shared the volume of customer messages, live chats, etc. There were distress calls from passengers on various tours, especially those impacted by abrupt lockdowns and in foreign lands. The call centre staff was at the front and centre of all such calls for help. The back-end teams worked with local, national and international authorities to ensure that the passengers were repatriated.'

As of mid-March, TUI Group suspended a vast majority of its travel operations, including holiday packages, cruises and hotel operations. Customers who had booked a plan/package with us were apprised of the situation and given the option of taking a future booking voucher or refund.

'While in good times, the focus is largely on how one can increase the bookings and get the maximum customers to successfully transact, we knew this was the time to focus on the information needs of the customers. Several customers were concerned about their bookings that were done earlier. We communicated with them through our social media channels, emails and phone calls to provide clarity on the status of their bookings. We prioritized our responses based on the customer's travel schedules. Customers who had a flight scheduled within the next 48 hours were addressed first,' Krishan tells me about TUI's approach.

The lockdown left many tourists stranded in different countries, including the crew and passengers on TUI cruises. The company had several discussions with the authorities such as embassies and the government, assuring them of quarantining the crew and the travellers in its own properties, wherever possible. The grounded aircrafts have been used to repatriate not just its own clients but also those of all travel operators who reached out to TUI for support.

'We worked with state and local authorities to safely disembark our crew and seafarers across the cruises. We got the required approvals and flew charters for European tourists who were visiting Goa. This was not the time to think about competition. People needed to get back home safely and wherever we had the means to do that, by virtue of our assets and partnerships with national and international tourism bodies, we did our best.'

TUI, like other travel operators, worked with partner airlines and hotels in getting cash refunds for its customers.

'Just an year and a half ago, TUI India had gone under a massive restructuring. Despite being part of a global company, we have been working as a start-up since this restructuring. The crisis has compounded the situation for the India business, especially as we depend on our parent company for a large source of our funding,' Krishan tells me.

On their front, the leaders are critically analysing every line in the P&L to look at ways of becoming more cost-efficient. Renegotiation of contracts is happening at global levels. Krishan tells me: 'An advantage of the restructuring has been that the India team is quite lean. Our cost is not linear to our revenue.'

One of the interesting angles of business continuity that Krishan shares in the story is how the plan included the contingency of the entire leadership falling sick and should that happen, the protocol that would be followed to keep the systems running. For a company of this scale and size, eminent risks like these can get brushed under the carpet or completely ignored.

'We tried to create redundancies in every function across the organization, right from our sourcing staff to the senior leadership. We asked ourselves what we should do if the entire management gets infected. These were difficult questions, but needed to be asked and prepared for.'

As the world is gradually opening up, TUI is taking baby steps in restarting its global operations. Globally, since the suspension of the programmes in mid-March, online enquiries have indicated that holidays remain important to its customers. The group has seen its customers committing for upcoming seasons. Following the recent easing of travel restrictions in Europe, the group has seen a notable increase in bookings for the summer holidays, with Germany and Belgium seeing strong recovery week on week. TUI restarted its summer season with two fully booked flights from Germany to Majorca (Spain). TUI's executive board, together with the operational management, is continuously evaluating the leisure travel policies and safety guidelines, and plans to manage its capacity depending on customer demand and in line with the specifications as well as requirements of the authorities in our source markets and destinations.

The organization is overhauling many of its operations to focus on the safety of travellers. Having implemented comprehensive health and safety protocols on-board the vessels, the company also plans to begin a gradual restart of the cruise business. TUI Cruises is planning to restart operations with short three- to four-day cruises this summer. The group is provisioning contactless check-ins at its hotels and ensuring social distancing for the guests in all common areas. Anti-viral disinfection is being carried out at regular intervals. The staff is working in fixed groups, so that in case of an infection, contact tracing is quick. The group's hotel chain RIU has recently launched RIU Protect, a new healthcare service for its customers. With this new service, which was developed with insurance support from AXA, RIU is offering medical care to its guests, including any affected by COVID-19 during their holidays.

'If you think, when 9/11 happened, airport security systems across the globe got overhauled. Expect similar ground-level changes to happen. From heat-sensing to on-the-spot rapid testing; from being able to pay a premium to sit alone in a row to drop in in-flight food consumptions; from contactless check-ins to staggered boarding—these landscape changes are here to stay.

'Our tourists travel in our own aircrafts, stay in our hotels and move around in our vehicles. Being vertically integrated helps us take controlled measures across the entire experience of the travellers.'

Speaking about the change in customer behaviour, Krishan tells how the demand for boutique properties, weekend getaways and homestays will increase as much as the share of prominent chains.

'Corporate travel is expected to decline worldwide. Even after the pandemic subsides, companies are unlikely to start making people travel as frequently. This will be seen as a big source of savings by the corporates and every travel will be scrutinized.

'For the rest of 2020, we anticipate a similar decline in leisure travel to international destinations, at least from India. Domestic travel, however, should recover sooner. People will prefer destinations closer to home which they can travel by road, in their own vehicles. Demand for boutique hotels and homestays will increase, as these allow social distancing. People will also not mind spending more to stay in luxurious properties, where they can be reasonably sure about the stringent safety protocols being followed.'

The crisis has prepared us to be open to any situation.

'Any action plan is short-lived. One needs to empathize with one's employees, customers as well as supply partners. The situation is impacting all of them as severely as it is impacting us. The lines are blurred of who can support whom. As I already mentioned, there is no place for competition,' Krishan says.

Yes, there is no place for competition.

About Krishan Singh

Krishan is the CEO and director of TUI India, a strong global leader in travel e-commerce. Krishan is known for change-management and starting up, turning around and scaling up businesses through a vision, with a special affinity for strategy, technology and a keen understanding of e-commerce. He has worked with start-ups as well as large global companies. He has outstanding market knowledge and commercial/strategic acumen in the travel and leisure sector.

Having led and executed successful implementation of artificial intelligence and machine learning, Krishan believes data is key for quick decision-making and e-commerce is a complex combination of stakeholders, employees, customers and vendor interests. He believes in a fair balance across these key interest groups and leading everyone towards a common goal through scalable technology. Leadership, in his opinion, is identifying the right talent and empowering them intelligently.

In his previous role at Yatra, where he had an eight-year stint, he was a member of the founding team for Yatra.com's hotels and holidays business and was part of the leadership team which saw the company get listed in NASDAQ. He also worked with Thomas Cook India to establish and grow their short haul business vertical and played a key role in establishing e-commerce and call centre sales channels.

Krishan is a graduate in commerce from Delhi University, with a post-graduate degree in tourism and travel management. He is also a mountaineering and trekking enthusiast and has spent several years exploring the Himalayas, including climbing three 6,000 plus metre peaks, before starting his corporate career.

LESSON 4

IMPORTANCE OF A BUSINESS CONTINUITY PLAN

Among the varied terms this pandemic has introduced to the world's vocabulary is also one which always existed but no one paid heed to it—the business continuity plan. I recollect being part of two such events in my corporate career, both of which needed the company to have a business continuity plan in place. First when I was working in a company that was severely cash crunched and every penny spent needed to be critically analysed. And the second one is the one every organization, including Google, built to prepare for the COVID pandemic.

Business continuity plans are often misconstrued as disaster recovery plans. Few leaders realize how the former is a proactive approach to avoiding and mitigating risks, while the latter is mostly about restoration and recovery post a disaster has already occurred.

Unfortunately, leaders either refuse to think that something could go wrong or massively wrong or have a vague notion of crisis response in their head or only consider a few, very specific, internal risks. Many leaders put together a plan based only on events that have occurred in the organization or externally. They lack foresight and do not have creative solutions to address eminent risks in today's connected world. A few leaders have a plan in place but the same is not demoed or tested on the floor. Doing the actual floor testing during the crisis renders the whole idea of having a plan meaningless. The highest level of maturity is achieved by those companies which have a plan and who get it periodically updated and extensively tested to ensure that it is sound and can be implemented whenever needed.

An important question here is: is it even possible to predict all the events that can happen to one's business? The answer is no. But if you think about the possibility of getting your entire workforce to work from home, the same could happen due to simple events such as a natural disaster, a war or disruptions such as public transportation strikes, contamination of the building, etc. In my own corporate experience, I have been part of two major fires in two different companies, which resulted in the workplaces being shut down. Be it ensuring an immediate safety of all the employees or the systemic plan for avoiding disruption to customers, both the companies were underprepared.

Research indicates that companies that proactively consider a contingency plan are the first to bounce back to business, often at the expense of competitors. A predefined business continuity plan combined with the proper insurance coverage, maximizes the chance of a successful recovery by eliminating hasty decision-making under stressful conditions.

It starts with an impact analysis and modelling various scenarios. The critical impacted components are employees, clients and the supply chain. Often, a business continuity plan needs a cross-functional leadership to come together and ensure organizational alignment around key objectives. It also needs to be phased, dealing with the most critical stuff first and then identifying medium- to long-term principles of thinking. In some cases, leaders also need to secure regulatory and compliance clearances. The plan also indicates the right level of frequency of monitoring progress and communicating to the different stakeholder groups.

Though the exact contents of these plans would vary by industry, company, scale and scope of the organization, no company is immune to the need of having such a plan in place.

Coming up with this plan needs the leaders to be forthcoming and brutally honest about asking difficult questions. I have heard leaders who make sure part of the plan is about what to do if those leaders themselves have a sudden exit or demise. It is an extremely uncomfortable thought but deserves to be tabled, when thinking of business continuity.

9

DUNZO

Dunzo is an e-commerce platform that is making hyperlocal transactions and supply chains more efficient through technology. It connects businesses across categories and empowers them with everything they need to grow their business—from driving orders, logistics and marketing, to inventory management, distribution and demand forecasting. For its users, Dunzo offers a full stack of services across commerce (groceries, restaurants, pet supplies, health and wellness), courier (pick-up and drop) and commute (bike taxi). Dunzo, which had its beginnings as a task-based WhatsApp group, has been the pioneer of hyperlocal courier and commerce in India. Standing strong at the forefront of innovation, Dunzo has been able to maintain its 'verb' status[1] by catering to an infinite number of use cases for its merchants, partners and customers. Dunzo has grown 50 times in the last two years, operating at 2 million monthly orders and growing 15 per cent month on month. Building efficiency across the supply chain, Dunzo's benchmark service is the leading factor for its growth and success. At an average delivery turnaround time of 24 minutes at under a dollar, the company is pushing micro-market profitability and building unparalleled customer experience. The company operates in Bengaluru, Pune, Delhi, Gurgaon, Hyderabad, Chennai, Mumbai and Jaipur. In the next 18 months (by 2021), Dunzo will be expanding to the top 20 cities in India. Dunzo's investors include Google, Blume Ventures, Aspada, Lightbox, STIC, 3L and Alteria Capital.

∼

---

[1]Verb status is often used to signify how users associate a company name with a particular action. Example: saying google instead of search or paytm instead of money transfer, etc.

I always wondered why somebody doesn't do something about that. Then I realized I was somebody.

—Lily Tomlin

Just as the word 'Google' has become synonymous with 'search', the word 'Dunzo' is becoming synonymous with home delivery. Be it a mother sending home-cooked food to a son stuck in a different part of the city or a friend sending a home-made birthday cake, Dunzo has become a prominent way to send things over to our family and friends. Be it ordering medicines from the nearby store or getting books delivered directly from a publisher's warehouse, the company is seeing newer use cases emerge during the pandemic. In a world where we are stepping out less and do not worry about paying a little extra for our safety and convenience, 'Dunzo it' will continue to remain our daily phrase.

Dunzo isn't a regular two-sided marketplace, rather a delivery partner. The three arms of Dunzo's business are its customers, partners and merchants/brand partners. The pandemic saw disruptions for all of these aspects. The customers wanted to get things on their doorsteps but without the risk of coming in contact with the delivery partner. The delivery partners needed to protect themselves as they made their living. The merchants were impacted by a frozen supply chain and shut shops due to lack of supplies and manpower. On the other hand, brands looked for means to directly reach the customers and looked to Dunzo for being able to establish that direct delivery channels. Here is how Dunzo navigated its way through the challenges and enabled smooth operations.

Kabeer Biswas, co-founder and chief executive officer (CEO) of Dunzo, tells me: 'When the government shut down flight and train services, we knew crazy times were ahead of us. When the lockdown was first announced, regulations of what fell under the essentials category varied for different states. For example, in Tamil Nadu, grocery delivery was considered an essential, but food delivery wasn't.

Regulations also changed, depending on locations and local authorities on ground. It took a few weeks for these directives to stabilize.'

The lockdown started seeing a surge in demand for grocery to be delivered. E-grocers were struggling to meet the surge in demand.

'We observed hoarding of essential food and grocery happen on our platform. Everything in the cart was being ordered in multiples. A customer who would usually order 5 kg of wheat was now ordering 20 kg. Customers started stocking oil, spices, ready-to-eats and non-perishables. People were piling up instant noodles and chocolates,' says Kabeer.

The platform was modified to prevent this hoarding. Quantity limits were placed in the app and customers were informed that this was being done in the larger interest of the community.

Dunzo's partners are its backbone and they get paid per order. The lockdown led to almost 30–40 per cent of the existing partners going to their villages and hometowns. On the other hand, there were people who did not have a means of income. By word of mouth, the company started getting many new on-boarding requests. Dunzo began remote on-boarding to bring in more partners. Earlier, these people would walk into the partner offices with their documents, and learn the workings on the go. During the lockdown, they sent all their documents online and were digitally trained on the partner app. The team also created a digital training on the safety protocols to be followed.

From partnering with other companies to help the partners rent bikes, to providing them COVID health insurance, the company ramped up its partners and ensured their stickiness on the platform. Masks, sanitizers and gloves were made available to these partners through the merchants and nearby stores.

'To ensure that the quality of service remains consistent, the team ensured that partners who are on-boarded digitally are not assigned complicated tasks. We assign them a few easy tasks before they take on complex ones.'

The complexity of every task went up as well. A simple task

such as picking up grocery and other items from a nearby store now entailed standing in longer queues and ensuring social distancing. Especially during the lockdown, the partners were stopped at various checkpoints and questioned on the tasks. Frequent regulatory changes and lack of clarity for ground officials added to the confusion. Sometimes, a store would shut down because of lack of supplies or manpower. And servicing the customers needed the partner to travel more than 20 km.

'On the legal side, we worked to get them authorized movement stickers and ensured their ID cards were digitally available on the app. We needed to work in close tandem with the authorities and ensure compliance. We introduced tips for our partners and reduced our payout time to them. We also sent daily reminders of health checks and tried to reduce the stigma around the virus. A silver lining was that with the lockdown and hence, deserted roads, the partners were able to serve more customers,' Kabeer shares.

On the merchant side, Kabeer talks about the trends and strategy the company has in the short to long term. There was an increase in store walk-in volumes and with the opening hour restrictions imposed by the local authorities, the need to prioritize walk-in customers and the lack of manpower to serve the demand, the delivery partner invariably needed to wait longer than earlier.

'In the short term, we supplied manpower to the local stores wherever they needed support. Order routing algorithms were fine-tuned to avoid 10 partners at one shop at the same time. In many cases, our partners actually drew circles outside shops for folks to maintain social distancing. We also reduced our payout time for easing the merchants' working capital.

'As our user acquisition cost is dropping and is near zero, we are now focusing on a merchant-first strategy. The top 15K general stores (by order volume) are crucial for our growth. We are aiming to deploy more manpower and deeper technology integrations for a near-real-time visibility into the inventory and demand management across in-store and online customers. We have helped these stores tie up with multiple suppliers and brands to ensure a larger supplier base and increased options,' Kabeer tells me.

On the technical front, not only was the technical infrastructure put under exponential stress, but the team needed to build flexible ways of ring-fencing areas for demand and supply as well as partner restrictions.

'Today a store was open. Tomorrow it came under a containment zone. Today a partner was allowed to deliver. Tomorrow he could be in the red zone. The platform needed to be nimble to all these use cases as well as have an easy way to do these configurations and a standardized communication for all such changes. Imagine a partner who is suddenly not allowed to deliver or a store not allowed to open. If they were not properly communicated, they would reach out to our call centres, putting load on the already stretched manpower.'

The crisis has also been an opportunity where Dunzo significantly scaled its partnerships with brands.

'Several brands have been eager to reach out and directly deliver to customers. Setting up the logistic infrastructure to do the same is not a core competence for many. We have provided them a storefront on our consumer app. FMCG brands such as Britannia, Coke, Pepsi, Nestle, Nivea, HUL, Bisleri, Cadbury, Dabur, etc. have seen a surge in organic demand through our platform. Right from ordering water to Hershey's chocolates, customers are seeing a variety of products not easily available in stores. Be it a 10 p.m. urge for Coke or a rush to deliver bread and butter, the use cases are varied. We have seen a surge in demand for not just food but also masks, sanitizers and detergents. People are ordering sexual wellness products as well as pregnancy kits. From diapers to pet supplies, people are shopping more frequently and across more categories.'

The company saw a surge of demand and downloads from areas where they hadn't been functioning.

'Internally, we were continuously working on opening up newer areas. But when you open the area, you need to have merchants on the platform for a good customer experience. If the user sees that the closest store is 9 km away, it isn't a great experience. This is why we increasingly focused on getting more distribution hubs of the brands on our platform. We worked to onboard more partners to be able to take on the additional demand.'

People who were already familiar with Dunzo are now ordering more through the app, while many are discovering the convenience it provides and becoming regular users. The company expects the users to stick around and be less price-sensitive, even as they begin to step out of their homes.

While Dunzo's partners have received appreciation for being on the front line, the company is also working on social initiatives to deliver essential services, free of cost, to elderly and differently abled people, impacted by the lockdown. In collaboration with several groups of volunteers, the company has delivered a range of commodities, from medicines and grocery to food. The company has also raised a contingency fund of approx. ₹60 lakh for the delivery partners, should they need financial or medical support.

What makes Dunzo stand apart is its quirky social media engagement. Right from Dunzo comics to light-hearted posts, the social media team is determined on spreading more joy, especially when the silver linings are rare to come by these days.

'We don't want to come across as someone who doesn't understand the gravity of the situation. But we also cannot change what we cannot change. And we need to create moments of happiness and be light-hearted in life. This is what the media team is intending to do through the communications.'

For a business seeing 30 times the growth in active users, 14 per cent revenue growth and three times the surge in essentials, the opportunities are huge. There is going to be drop in some of the categories, especially as the country opens up, but at a strategic level, the Dunzo team is hopeful to turn profitable soon.

About Kabeer Biswas

Kabeer Biswas is the co-founder and chief executive officer (CEO) of Dunzo.

Hailing from the town of Silvassa, in the Indian Union Territory of Dadra and Nagar Haveli, Kabeer earned his B.E. in computer engineering from the University of Mumbai in 2004. He followed this up with an MBA from SVKM's Narsee Monjee Institute of Management Studies (NMIMS) in Mumbai. After graduating, Kabeer went on to join Bharti Airtel Limited in 2007, where he handled sales and products. During his tenure with the telecom giant, Kabeer would gain valuable experience in building products for scale, understanding the root problem and building solutions for them, as well as understanding ground operations. He founded his first venture, Hoppr, a location-based mobile service offering check-ins, coupons and location-aware services in India. Later acquired by Hike Messenger, Hoppr paved the way for Kabeer to get back to the drawing board once again. This gave way to Dunzo Digital Pvt. Ltd Kabeer started Dunzo in 2015 as a way to curtail his own to-do list. Kabeer's WhatsApp chats were flooded with requests and the number of users grew organically and exponentially. It was time to scale up and that's how the Dunzo app came to be.

10

IXIGO

ixigo operates as an intelligent, artificial intelligence (AI)-based travel app for deal discovery, personalized recommendations, airfare predictions, train delay information, passenger name reservation (PNR) confirmation predictions and for providing fully automated customer service over chat and voice. In 2019, ixigo became India's most used travel app with a user base of over 170 million travellers. In April 2020, ixigo was recognized in the top 100 Asia-Pacific high-growth companies by the Financial Times, UK. FT ranks ixigo as the third fastest growing travel and leisure company in Asia-Pacific.

∽

To get customers, you need to go from the heart to the brain to the wallet.

—Gary Vaynerchuk

It was one of ixigo's marketing videos that caught my attention. The travel safety video, based on the Super Mario Brothers game[1], was one of the 10 videos that ixigo had created as part of its public awareness campaign for safe travel amidst the pandemic. Each of these videos made me feel nostalgic about travel while also educating me about the need to travel safely.

I had already interviewed TUI India's leadership for my book and debated whether to include two stories from the same sector

---

[1] https://www.youtube.com/watch?time_continue=4&v=Bc83dXxYYhA&feature=emb_logo

(travel) in the book. 'Won't it be a repetition for the book?' I asked myself. However, having researched more about ixigo, I realized that the two stories and their leadership challenges were unique in their own ways.

While there were common challenges, there were also diversities. While one was a global company, the other largely served Indian customers. While one was known for its vertical integration, the other was an AI first. The differences were diverse enough for both the stories to provide their own unique leadership lessons. I decided to go ahead with interviewing the ixigo founders, Aloke Bajpai and Rajnish Kumar.

Aloke and Rajnish worked in a European travel company before starting off on their own. ixigo survived the financial crisis of 2007–08 and has seen several ups and downs in the sector, especially when interntional airlines such as Frontier Airlines suddenly declared bankruptcy.

The ixigo founders saw this present-day crisis coming since March.

'Back in early March, when the first cases of COVID were reported in India, we mentally prepared ourselves that at some point there would be a lockdown. We chalked out Plan B and braced ourselves for zero revenues at least for six months after the lockdown. We debated whether to let our staff go or find a way to retain them and see this through together. We agreed that we should make a collective sacrifice. We had done this before in 2008; we didn't let people go then, but got them on half-compensation for nine months.'

The leadership made sure everyone still got a certain percentage of their salary. The founders took home zero salaries. The leadership took a 60–80 per cent pay cut, the rest of the company a 20–50 per cent pay cut and under a certain threshold, there was no cut.

It was a timely foresight to do this because for the next two months, there were no transactions. For the first time, Indian Railways, the lifeline of India, which ferried over 20 million passengers every day (figure for 2019–20), completely stopped operations.[1] Trains and flights were the best pair of legs of the business and the impact was felt immediately.

The sudden announcement of the nationwide lockdown caught many unawares. This was also the time when the call centre teams started working from home. In business-as-usual scenarios, the customer care teams and call centre executives operate from physical office spaces. They did not carry their laptops home. In fact, most of them do not even have a laptop, but work on their desktops. The sudden lockdown left ixigo with very little time to procure and hand them new machines. The leadership prioritized handling this with technology.

'For three weeks, almost all our staff worked in customer service. Within a day, our site had a COVID information centre. This was one central place where customers could come and get their queries answered. Right from the process of rescheduling and cancellations to the policies of every airline, everything was updated for customers to read through and be self-empowered rather than needing to reach us. We personalized the information page so that instead of having to read through 20 different policies to figure out which one applied to you, we took you straight to those that were applicable to you.

'We trained Tara, our AI-based chat assistant, and developed a new version in early March. Tara saved us a lot of customer support anxiety by addressing 70 per cent of our queries. This helped us manage the incoming load on operations, while doing the optimal thing for the customers.'

Product features like these never get prioritized in an industry where valuations are based on top lines. These are not the most critical things on the road map, as these are not scenarios every customer goes through. But COVID threw prioritization out of the window.

---

[1]'Indian Railways Celebrates 167th Birthday Without Running Any Trains,' *The Indian Express*, 17 April 2020, https://indianexpress.com/article/india/indian-railways-celebrates-167th-birthday-without-running-any-trains-6366650/, last accessed on 9 December 2020.

'Does the old road map exist? Sure, it does. But the priorities have changed overnight. We have shifted our focus from bookings to rescheduling and change requests. From offers and promotions, we have moved to information communication in tones appropriate for such times. From bookings, we have shifted to customer engagement. From ticket size, we have shifted to customer lifetime value.'

Were there other sources of revenue coming at this time for ixigo?

'Fortunately, we had revenues from advertisements on our mobile travel properties. (Pre-COVID, ixigo had 30 million monthly users!) We did continue monetizing from that, as there was still traffic coming in for information.

'We did a rally call to our team: let's build something more relevant for our customers. From that, we launched our COVID Centre, on our train and flight app, which informed people where to get tested and the nearest facilities they could avail of. For that, we tied up with pharmaceutical and testing centres. The content was more suited for health as well as what to do during lockdown, such as entertainment content. We developed that in two weeks and we managed to retain half the traffic for April and May.'

Travel opened up in the third week of May and ixigo's transactions settled at 25 per cent of pre-COVID levels. What has resumed is essential travel, non-discretionary demand for unavoidable circumstances and family/personal reasons. International travel, on the other hand, is going to get significantly hit and is predicted to have a much longer recovery horizon. During such times, ixigo is heavily focused on customer engagement without spending any marketing money.

ixigo's social media team is trying to create a positive spirit in the minds of the customers. Their earliest video campaign during this crisis had the most popular travel destinations paired with thematic Bollywood songs to create nostalgia in the hearts of the viewers.[1] They

---

[1] https://www.ixigo.com/take-a-virtual-trip-with-these-top-bollywood-songs-story-1149374, last accessed on 4 December 2020.

also produced a 'Sounds We Miss' video, which was a collection of sounds of travel to remind people of what they were missing during lockdown.[1] The most recent one, based on the Super Mario game, reminds people of staying safe while travelling.

'All these videos have gone viral and helped us keep our customers connected, without spending a single penny on digital advertising. Aashish Chopra, who heads our content marketing, has written a book on it, *Fast, Cheap & Viral*. I have daily meetings with our Content staff and we brainstorm on viral marketing. The thing is, no idea is a bad one; sometimes we just end up cracking jokes, but at times, we come up with brilliant ideas and execute them fast. Over time, we have developed an understanding of what works and what doesn't for the different platforms. We don't hire professional actors. Instead, we hold auditions for in-house talent, where ixigems (ixigo employees) can participate and contribute to our marketing campaigns.'

The ixigo founders pride themselves in their culture, where everyone works as a team and ideas from all quarters are appreciated, irrespective of the designation. These are times when the hierarchical boundaries of the company can work as an impediment. Rajnish and Aloke ensure that their company does not have such a culture. In the time of this crisis, the founders gave 2.3 per cent of the company as deeply discounted employee stock ownership plans (ESOPs) to its employees to foster the culture of ownership and reward people for sticking around.

These are times when every day seems worse than the previous one. The founders stress on the importance of being transparent.

'Great cultures and companies are built on the pillars of transparency. Crises such the fall of SpiceJet, Air India and Jet Airways have hit our industry hard. It is important to communicate not just upstream, with the board but even downstream, with the

---

[1] https://www.youtube.com/watch?v=am-8LWXeJsY, last accessed on 4 December 2020.

employees and supply partners. Even when you cannot honour your commitments to them, be transparent, be vulnerable. Do not act as if you know it all, when the reality is you don't. Seek help and advice and you will be surprised with what comes your way.'

Aloke also makes a great point when he says that this period can act as a litmus test for the employees.

'There are employees who up their game and start thinking of ways to get out of a crisis, rather than being stuck in it. There are also employees who work only for money and get insecure and start disrespecting the company's values. Leaders should use these times to be observant. Just observe them as humans, before you judge them as employees.'

Aloke is optimistic that this too shall pass. He cautions how human beings overreact, not just to downsides but also to upsides. He is hopeful this too shall pass and the company will sail through. The key is to survive the next 12 months and come out shining on the other side.

About Rajnish Kumar and Aloke Bajpai

Rajnish Kumar is the co-founder and chief technology officer (CTO) of ixigo, an intelligent AI-based travel app. Spearheading the company's innovation and technology, he has created many global industry-first products that are revolutionizing the way India travels. Under his leadership, ixigo trains app has emerged as the sixth most downloaded travel app globally and the second most downloaded travel app in India.[1] He holds a B.Tech degree in computer science from the Indian Institute of Technology (IIT), Kanpur. He has also published research papers on AI, one of which was presented at

---

[1] IANS, 'ixigo 6th Most Downloaded Travel App Globally,' *Business Standard*, 28 March 2018, https://www.business-standard.com/article/news-ians/ixigo-6th-most-downloaded-travel-app-globally-119032800727_1.html, last accessed on 9 December 2020.

Massachusetts Institute of Technology (MIT), Boston in 2004.

Aloke Bajpai is ixigo's co-founder and chief executive officer (CEO). A travel industry veteran, he has worked in various product and technology roles at Amadeus, France, prior to launching ixigo in 2007. Under his leadership, ixigo has become the most innovative and fastest-growing app in the travel segment.

A big supporter of entrepreneurship, Aloke is a key investor and advisor for several start-ups and accelerators. An IIT Kanpur alumnus and MBA graduate from INSEAD, he loves discovering new cultures, creative writing, reading history and collecting gadgets.

LESSON 5

EMPLOYEE WELL-BEING

'We think of our shareholders as food—it's essential, but you can live without it for a few days; our customers are like water, again a necessity, but you can survive a couple of days without it; our employees are like air, we live and breathe by them,' Sanket Atal, managing director, Intuit India.

I came across this powerful quote and truly believe in its essence. The single biggest common thread across all my conversations with senior leaders was about how much the leaders cared for and prioritized employee well-being. It was not just about keeping them physically safe but also ensuring people adjusted well to working from home. The uncertain business environment and isolation at home have had mental implications, which need attention at the highest levels.

Essential front-line workers are much more exposed physically. Leaders have been prioritizing safety training, provisions of safety gears to these workers and ensuring they are adequately covered under insurance schemes. In many of my stories, the front-line workers were unable to meet their families for months at end and lived in constant fear of not just getting infected but also risking their near ones.

Well-intentioned people were unable to work from home. Someone was staying in a small space with their families, making it difficult to concentrate. Someone else was taking care of the kids and family, in the absence of any support. Some have had their immediate family infected by the virus. Employees were feeling guilty for not being able to give their 100 per cent. They were working odd hours and their sleep schedules were disturbed. Beyond keeping people physically protected, the top priority of every leader has been to ensure that the employees are able to manage the exhaustion and burn-out that results from long periods of working from home.

While it may sound obvious, crises are crises because people suffer. In a situation where emotions and anxieties run high, leaders connected with employees and other stakeholders, and acknowledged the personal and professional challenges they were going through. Impactful leaders conveyed their vision in a manner that the employees were aligned, motivated and rallied against.

Effective crisis management requires integrity, accountability and moral courage. Thoughtful, frequent and empathetic communication signals that the leaders in my book shared with their organization showed that they cared and were together in the journey that each employee was going through. These messages were delivered with 'bounded optimism', hope combined with realism. Leaders sent positive messages but resisted the temptation to conceal bad news and take an overconfident, upbeat tone. Showing excessive confidence and optimism in spite of obviously difficult or even deteriorating conditions raises suspicion and mistrust.

11

FAMILY OF DISABLED

Family of Disabled (FOD) is a registered voluntary organization which has been serving people with disabilities since 1992. Being a cross-disability organization, FOD is able to serve people with different disabilities. Founded by Dr Rajinder Johar after he became quadriplegic from a gunshot injury to his spine, FOD aims at building and nurturing the capacities of disabled persons and assisting them in becoming self-reliant.

FOD has several programmes to serve specific needs of people with disabilities—from education sponsorship to sustainable employment generation, physical rehabilitation and creative nurturing. FOD also regularly distributes aids and appliances to people with disabilities and runs an annual arts exhibition titled 'Beyond Limits', which showcases the works of talented disabled artists from across the country. It is also engaged in the space of corporate gifting and offers hand-made products by disabled artists. Unnati is FOD's multipurpose rehabilitation centre that provides life skill training to disabled people.

All the programmes of FOD are a result of a deeper and more sensitive, and not just superficial understanding of disability. The organization has received 27 awards for its services, including three national awards. Till date, FOD does not receive any grant or aid from the government. For more information on FOD, visit www.familyofdisabled.org.

∽

Unless someone like you cares a whole awful lot, nothing is going to get better. It's not.

—Dr Seuss

COVID-19 has exposed the grim inequalities in our country. While there is a class like us, who can stay comfortably in our homes and flood our Instagram accounts with pictures of exotic dishes we are cooking, there is a class we have bracketed under the term 'migrant labourers'. We read about them in the newspapers or hear about them in the news; we even feel guilty for some time, but then move on with our day. There is another class of people that has been pushed to obscurity. They too have been rendered jobless and homeless by this pandemic. They cannot see, hear, speak, walk or even wash their hands frequently as they don't have any. FOD is a family of these differently abled.

I have been associated with FOD since 2013. I interviewed the founder of the organization, Rajinder Johar. Rajinder sir had been bedridden for more than 30 years of his life and ran this organization through a support group. Before his death in 2018, he passed on the baton to his daughter, Preeti Johar. Amidst her father's death, the birth of her son and her mother's battle with cancer, Preeti had enough reasons to abandon the cause. And yet, she did not. Organizations such as FOD take years to build donors' trust. Most donors trust the founder and give their valuable contributions. It took a while for Preeti to regain that trust. And just when she was all set to lead, COVID happened.

FOD conducted its annual fundraising event in March this year.

'March is the time when most organizations and individuals who want to make donations to avail tax exemptions are very active. We partner with GiveIndia platform for fundraising. Depending on how much money we are able to raise, GiveIndia also contributes and it introduces different schemes of rewarding each year in order to encourage fundraising efforts made by the NGOs,' Preeti tells me.

These funds are used across several initiatives throughout the year. FOD disburses aids and appliances to the differently abled, subsidizes education and provides funds to set up small businesses.

'We believe in empowering people, instead of making them dependent on us. We do project-based fundraising, where donors are fully aware of where their money is being utilized. In fact, our donors are specific about where they would want to contribute. Some donors donate to employment-generation projects/initiatives, some to the procurement of wheelchairs and other equipment, and others to promote differently abled artists. But all our donations are project-based.'

Things completely changed after COVID. Soon after the first lockdown was declared, the government announced several schemes for providing food to the poor and needy. FOD's ground workers informed Preeti about the realities for the differently abled people.

While a normal person could stand in queues for their rations, what about someone who cannot stand on their feet? What about someone who cannot see, or hear, or speak? There were several instances of the police lathi-charging the crowds to dispel them. There was a lot of commotion. There were wheelchair-bound, blind, deaf and mute people in these queues.

'In a world of social distancing, no one was ready to hold a blind person's hand and take them to get their free ration. When volunteers reached the hearing impaired people, they found that the inability to communicate had left many hungry. The masks are also an obstruction for the hearing impaired person to read lips. The procedure to get an e-coupon, while it was online, was not accessible to someone who could not see. Many people did not have phones or the internet to fill this form.'

FOD started working with legal experts and policymakers to make the necessary adjustments for the differently abled. They also procured movement passes for its ground staff and trained them to help the differently abled procure their essential supplies while keeping themselves safe. From filling their application forms to door-step delivery of essentials and medicines, the team innovated on the ground to solve these special needs.

'We worked at several levels in the bureaucratic hierarchies and sensitized the authorities on the needs of the differently abled. These are people who cannot move on their own. Even in red zones and containment zones, volunteers needed to visit these people in their homes. They had special dietary requirements that needed to be catered to. These people needed more than just food. They were heavily dependent on medicines and our volunteers made sure that these reached them on time. FOD is working with connecting local volunteers in these zones, so that the travel need is minimized.'

FOD also collaborated with the Blind Relief Association and started providing ration kits to the differently abled already registered with them as well as to those who were referred through reliable contacts. They started reaching out proactively to people who they were certain they would need help.

'This was the first time we started accepting food as donations. Our community workers were our pulse and kept us honest about the day-to-day ground situations as they emerged.'

In this pandemic, a lot of bedridden people had their caretakers not being able to come to take care of them.

'Imagine a bedridden person whose life is completely dependent on his caretaker. Right from their washroom needs, to eating and even being put to bed, they need support. The caretakers were also scared to step out of their homes. The differently abled too were scared of being exposed through their caretakers. In certain cases, where the caretaker could not stay with these people, we arranged passes for them. In other cases, we sensitized the caretakers of the needs of their employer and how they could keep themselves, and the person they are taking care of, safe. FOD also provided diapers, gloves, disposable masks, etc. for such patients,' Preeti shares with me.

FOD also saw cases where people were not able to get their usual physiotherapy because hospitals were closed or operating in limited capacities or converted into COVID hospitals.

'It has been a nightmare for the differently abled, who have had to run from pillar to post to get the much-needed regular medical check-ups. You cannot keep getting COVID tests done before being treated. It is infeasible, cost-prohibitive and life-threatening. Through our network of doctors, lawyers and donors, we continue to deal with these cases individually and put the required pressures on hospitals to get the due medical attention for these people.'

In all of this, FOD's own staff too was very scared initially to come to work. Moreover, some of their projects such as cutting, tailoring and pencil making were not seeing demand.

'FOD employs the differently abled. We did not have sufficient demand for the products they were making. I retrained a few of them to the needs of the present situation. From making bags, we started making masks. From making pencils, we started accounting and auditing the ration kits we were providing, so that refills were easy and did not need the beneficiary to reach us again. Since it was risky to ask them to come to work, we encouraged the tailoring unit to take the machines home and make masks. We alternated our staff so that at any given point in time, our home office was not crowded,' Preeti tells me about how FOD adapted to the situation.

Preeti shares a sad anecdote around a schizophrenic person she employed. She had asked the person not to come to work as she was unable to find a suitable task for him. Soon the person started having panic attacks at home. Despite being paid in full, the person requested Preeti to give him some work. He even confessed of having tendencies to harm his family members, if he was made to stay longer at home.

'While we ask people to stay at home, people with mental disabilities need to be kept engaged. Their routine life keeps them sane. Longer periods of confinement are a risk to their mental well-being,' Preeti explains.

While FOD had promised to get him back by the first week of June and find a suitable work for him, this case also led Preeti to work with counsellors who have been offering their support to people with mental disabilities and their families.

FOD has helped more than a thousand differently abled and their families in surviving through the crisis. It is bracing itself for the aftereffects of the pandemic that are here to stay.

'The pandemic has reduced previous income levels. While it

will take a long time for all the poor people to rehabilitate, the road will be much longer for those of us who are physically and mentally impaired. Till then, as an organization, we have pivoted from empowering them to making sure they can survive through these times,' Preeti says.

Fortunately, there is a silver lining in all of this. Preeti's work on ground is giving her donors the confidence that the organization will continue its founder's legacy even if he is not around.

'Earlier, donors wanted to donate only to special causes. If a donor was attached to the cause of employment, they would not donate to the cause of education. If a donor wanted to help someone by giving them food, they would not be ready to donate for medicines. But in this pandemic, they tell me I have full authority and liberty to use the funds as I deemed fit. I make sure I keep them posted, as transparency helps strengthen trust.'

FOD is not a business organization. Yet, their challenges are not any different—whether it is about the cash crunch, or keeping one's donors (read investors) engaged or ensuring employee safety, especially those on the front line. Preeti's leadership is providing hope to many. They are not in the business of making money, but they are in the business of saving lives.

'I am playing it by ear, Disha,' Preeti confides. 'If this stays for longer, we may not have the funds to monetarily help people. We still have our network through which we can get donations in kind that can be further disbursed. We also continue to educate and sensitize people around the special needs of the differently abled. We will continue to be their voice.'

FOD has trained the differently abled to produce masks and is working with corporates to set up a self-sustaining model and keep the systems running. Even when the world regains 'normalcy' for the able-bodied like us, it will take a long time for the world to be normal again for those of us who are physically or mentally impaired. The road to recovery is long and dark for this section of society. But I am hopeful, years down the line, FOD would have helped thousands of lives to emerge stronger from the crisis.

About Preeti Johar

Preeti Johar is the chief executive officer (CEO) of FOD. Her growing-up years were unlike most of us. Rajinder Johar, her father, was bedridden for life. Her mother was too occupied making ends meet. No one could accompany her to the park. No one could teach her to cycle. Preeti spent her time at home in her father's room. She picked up the workings of FOD, sitting there and observing the functioning from her father's bed.

Along with her uncle Surinder Johar, she devised a writing device, which their father tied to his wrist and started writing with the help of shoulder movements. Since both the children got involved with him in this work early in childhood, it started reflecting in their character. After completing her school, as Mr Johar's health started deteriorating and his concern regarding the enormous work he was doing bothered him too much, Preeti decided to take the plunge and join her father full time.

Since the last 20 years, Preeti has been working with the mission of serving disabled people. In 2018, she formally took over the role of the CEO of the organization when her father left for his heavenly abode. Under her leadership, the organization has been growing and expanding its impact into more areas and districts across Delhi. Preeti is a young leader and recipient of several awards and recognitions for the work she has been doing for the disabled community.

12

BRIGADE METROPOLIS RWA

Brigade Metropolis, Bengaluru is a meticulous project by the Brigade Group. This well-designed project has 1,608 residential units spread across 12 towers. The society is cosmopolitan, with a large part of its residents having people from across the country. The residents work in varied sectors and have diverse opinions on issues related to the society. The residential community annually elects a group of 25 representatives from among the residents to take care of various aspects of the society's management, including horticulture, cultural activities, water, gas, sewage treatment, cleaning and maintenance. Brigade Metropolis has won the best 'Residential Property South' at the CNBC Awaaz CRISIL CREDAI Real Estate Awards 2010.

~

In crisis management, be quick with the facts, slow with the blame.

—Leonard Saffir

This is not a business organization. Nor is this a not-for-profit. This is not a formal organization. Nor is this an organization many would have heard of. This is an association that works for the welfare of its residents, commonly known as the RWA.

Why would an RWA feature in a book focused on leadership in crisis? What leadership lessons can it possibly contain? Where does it fare with the likes of the other stories in this book?

As I witnessed the crisis unfold from the comfort of my home, I have seen the leadership of this organization up close and personal. I have seen how one can influence without authority, react to an ever-evolving situation sometimes by consensus and sometimes with a few leaders vetoing in time-sensitive situations. The beauty of this story is the fact that there are no founders of the company involved and every leader is also a resident. So one's decisions don't just impact the resident community but also one's next-door neighbour and even one's own family. There are situations when opinions are divided between families, neighbours and there is an urge to comply, to maintain relationships. Leading in such times, keeping the interest of everyone in mind while also doing one's full-time corporate job and helping in household work demands an intrinsic motivation and commitment.

Brigade Metropolis, the community I live in, houses 1,600 plus families and 5,000 plus individuals. The entire administration of the community is run by a set of 25 individuals elected every year by the residents. There is a secretary for each of the 12 blocks, people leading housekeeping, sewage treatment, technical maintenance, security, horticulture, sports and cultural efforts, treasurers, secretary, vice president and president. The management committee works with outsourced vendors in their respective areas. Joining the committee is purely voluntary and no payouts are made in any form.

The first society-level decision around the pandemic was made in March 2020, when the committee decided not to celebrate Holi. The residents have always looked forward to the festival and every year they would celebrate it together—playing with colours and water. The decision was seen by many as a panic reaction and people voiced their dissent on the society social forums.

Manoj Mahur, the secretary, tells us: 'We met and formed a crisis management task force. The committee felt that this would need a significant mindshare for the next few weeks and hence it was important that the task force consisted of fewer people who could dedicate more time and take quick decisions, when needed. The committee would put their weight behind these decisions and give the task force full autonomy to communicate with the residents.'

Given that each of the team members also had a corporate job to take care of, the team would meet either early in the day or late in the evening. Decisions were taken by only those who joined these meetings.

Many of the residents had been travelling abroad and were now returning to the community. This posed a serious risk to the entire community. In order to ensure safety of all the residents, the team decided to home quarantine the returning residents for 14 days.

'The returning residents were not happy. Some of them felt they were being unnecessarily singled out. We needed to ensure that: i) we made it easy for the residents to stay indoors by delivering everything they needed to their doorsteps; ii) we helped take care of their mental well-being; iii) we avoid panic in the society, especially among neighbours of people who were home quarantined.

'We formed a group of volunteers and connected them with the quarantined residents over WhatsApp. This was used for people to place their orders and volunteers delivered things at their doorsteps. The volunteers also called the residents to ensure they were keeping healthy, both physically and mentally. The volunteers tried to assuage any stigma in the minds of these residents, while strictly telling them to be indoors. We also educated the rest of the community that the people indoors were not COVID patients and that we should applaud them, instead of seeing them as a potential risk.'

The committee tallied its data with the data from the government and found out a few people who had not declared their travel and had not quarantined themselves. The team engaged these people in conversation and in some severe cases of non-compliance, reached out to authorities for help.

'We had no intention of getting anyone fined. We only wanted to deter people from violating these community rules.'

The committee deliberated on whether the names of the quarantined people should be made public to the rest of the community. This would help the neighbours keep a watch and alert the committee in case of any violations. However, there was also sensitivity around people's privacy. Moreover, that may have deterred people from declaring their status in the first place. The task force was divided in this matter. Manoj decided to go with what he felt was appropriate in the situation. He declared the list on the community forum, while reinforcing the need to be kind and empathetic.

'Every time I stepped outside my home, someone or the other would stop me and share their opinion. I was trying to keep calm and maintained silence when I felt it could lead to a toxic or futile conversation.'

When the prime minister announced the nationwide Janata curfew and followed it up with the lockdown, there was a need to ensure the same was followed by the residents as well.

'The first thing was about understanding the implications of the lockdown at a community level. The second thing was to connect with other RWAs to understand their plan of action. And the third was to implement what was right for us. Given our size and uniqueness, we had a major voice in the Bangalore Apartment Federation. But each community was unique. Some housed a lesser number of people and also had a smaller acreage. Ours was a community that not only housed many families but also was spread over a much larger area. The upkeep, security and maintenance needed significant manpower. Simple things such as allowing people from outside to come and do the regular sewage treatment became crucial, in the light of safety and compliance concerns. A lot of the housekeeping staff went to their villages. We debated on how to incentivize the rest to stay back, so that our plants were well maintained, garbage collected and security did not suffer,' Manoj tells me.

There were several questions that the task force discussed, debated and consulted other RWAs and local authorities on: should we allow walking inside the campus? What about going out? Should we keep track of who is coming in or going out? Should we allow visitors? What about allowing household help, maids and cooks? How would we monitor and deter non-compliance?'

These decisions may seem trivial, but they impacted the everyday living of people, most of whom were working from home by then.

The task force met every day and took these decisions. The team also communicated these decisions to the residents on a real-time basis, explaining the rationale behind them. Of course, in a community of 1,600 plus families, opinions were divided. Social forums were filled with debates, toxic conversations questioning the decisions of the task force and making recommendations. People pointed fingers at each other and lines of civility were often crossed in expressing one's opinions. In all this, Manoj and his team maintained their decorum and continued to communicate in a strict yet empathetic tone over regular email notices.

'The team and I would get personal messages, but we ignored these and focussed on our work. We also had our day jobs as well as household work to do. If we started responding to each of such accusations, it would be impossible to work,' says Manoj, and rightly so.

The team also worked with the grocery store within the campus to ensure that social distancing protocols were put in place.

'The store had a shortage of staff. Some of us personally helped the store in procuring supplies. We negotiated with the nearest branch of METRO cash-and-carry and ensured our stores were never short of supply and their stock request was fulfilled in a short time. We also have the franchise of a chain in our campus. We spoke to its regional manager to ensure adherence to safety protocols. When we got to know that the Horticultural Producers Co-operative Marketing and Processing Society (HOPCOMS) was starting an initiative of door-to-door delivery of fresh fruits and vegetables, we struck a partnership with them, wherein trucks would come to our society and residents could get fresh grocery at best prices without having to step out of the society.'

When the team saw the residents relying on online deliveries, dedicated areas near the main gate were set up to ensure the delivery agents did not visit all the buildings and social distancing could be monitored at one aggregation point. When people began to delay their pick-ups from these points, light penalties were imposed to avoid packages being piled up at these drop points. The back gate was closed and all entries and exits were concentrated at the front gate, where logs of all people coming in and going out were maintained. Everyone coming in was mandatorily made to sanitize one's hands.

In all of this, it was also important to have proactive protocols, should a positive case be reported in the society. The team set these standard operating procedures (SOPs) well ahead. So when a person who had travelled abroad reported some symptoms, the team already knew whom to contact, how to get the test done, which blocks to seal, what areas to sanitize and so on. Thankfully the person tested negative. But I personally observed the team calming the residents while doing their due diligence.

The team planned several initiatives to build a bond between the residents. People were asked to stand in their balconies and clap for the guards and housekeeping staff. A social initiative was started to provide food to the security staff, who, by then, were made to stay within the campus for their safety and especially since the mode of transport was restricted in the lockdown. The team urged residents to continue paying salaries to the support staff as they were reliant on us for their livelihoods. The team also stepped above and beyond their commitment to support social initiatives for migrant labourers. Food cooked and packed by the residents as well as packed food from the market were given to a partner non-governmental organization (NGO), who distributed the same at migrant labourer camps and at bus and railway stations. The elderly residents of the society were provided all the support they needed so that they did not have to step out of their homes and for this volunteer groups were formed. People not only brought them essential supplies but even cooked food and did video conversations with their neighbours.

As the lockdown was eased, the team continued to review its decisions and make amends as and when needed. Towards the end of June, the community reported its first case. By then, the cases in Bengaluru had been significantly rising and shortcomings of the healthcare infrastructure of the city had begun to hurt it. The established SOPs and the diverse network of the community not only helped in getting optimal medical attention for the patient but also ensured community support was put in place for the immediate impacted family as well as the neighbouring houses that needed to be quarantined.

With the passage of time and the easing of government regulations, the team decided to gradually lift the restrictions but cautioned the residents to self-monitor. The society celebrated festivals such as Janamashtami, Independence Day and Ganesh Chaturthi while maintaining social distancing. The team also procured oxygen concentrators, should the need arise.

As fatigue sets in, people are likely to be more lax. The committee is well-aware of the criticality of the work they are doing in keeping everyone safe. As Manoj reaffirms, '*You* are the key to keep Brigade Metropolis safe.'

About Manoj Mahur

Manoj Mahur is currently Digital Delivery Lead at EXL Service, an MNC with 26,000 employees across the globe. He has over 18 years of experience in information technology (IT) programme management and digital deliveries. He has worked with EXL as Project Manager, Programme Manager and Delivery Lead in different functional areas such as financials, supply chain, travel and logistics. Before that, he worked with a US-based start-up for 7 years as Team Lead and Project Manager for their supply chain module.

Manoj formerly served as Secretary, Brigade Metropolis Resident Welfare Association and is now its president.

LESSON 6

RISING ABOVE SELF-INTEREST

'There is nothing noble in being superior to your fellow man; true nobility is being superior to your former self,' said Ernest Hemingway.

What makes a leader is not just thinking about self but for the larger community. 'Self' in this context is the leader's organization. In times of crisis, it is easy to get sucked into what may work for one's organization. But situations like these are also when leaders step up for their communities. Be it giving back to the community in cash or kind or even gestures where one takes care of people who are not directly on the organization's payroll but on the front line; different leaders have showcased how it is not enough if the organization alone progresses. Not one leader I spoke to saw crisis as a time to carve out a competitive advantage; definitely not at the cost of a struggling competitor.

ACT FiberNet provided free internet to isolation camps. Urban Company and many other companies got insurance done for their partners. Shapoorji Pallonji Group housed their labourers at their sites, taking care of their food and healthcare needs. Delhi Police had several examples where officers wrote poetry and sang songs to keep the morale of the citizens high. The story of TUI where they repatriated not just their own clients but also of their competitors or anyone who reached out to them is commendable. Manish Tripathi, who we talk about later in this book, could have continued producing creative designs for India's and the world's elitists. Yet, he chose the difficult path of starting an employment chain in the country by manufacturing masks. Zerodha founders personally went out on the streets to distribute food. Acts like these speak about leadership.

Compassion is leadership, leadership is compassion: compassion not just for those close to us but for the community and people unrelated to us. If anything, the crisis will make leadership more humane and above self-interest.

13

YOURNEST VENTURE CAPITAL

YourNest Venture Capital is an early stage venture capital fund that invests in deep tech-enabled 'Pre-Series A' start-ups in India. The key focus areas are enterprise SaaS (Software as a Service) businesses, especially in the deep tech domain: artificial intelligence/machine learning, Distributed Ledger Technologies, Cloud Offerings, Developer Tools, Robotics, Hardware, Industrial internet-of-things (IoT), Robotic Process Automation Software, Wearables and Augmented Reality/Virtual Reality/ Mixed Reality. YourNest receives an average of 75 new proposals every week, across industries and domains.

Its portfolio companies include Miko (edutainment companion robot), CRON Systems (plugs the gap between complex 3D Sensors and real-world applications), virtual reality start-up SmartVizX, an EdTech VFX start-up 3rdFlix, fintech start-up CredRight, visual enhancement start-up, Orbo AI and many more. Most recently, YourNext exited from Uniphore and recorded a sevenfold return.

∼

The winner is the chef who takes the same ingredients as everyone else and produces the best results.

—Edward de Bono

Swiggy laid off 1,100 employees on 19 May 2020. A day later, Ola announced that it was laying off 1,400 of its people. In the first three months of the pandemic, every morning I would pick up the newspaper, I would learn of the damaging effect of this pandemic on the start-up ecosystem. Companies that had been there for years now; companies which had become an everyday use case for us; companies that were expanding aggressively not just in India but across the globe, were suddenly staring at losses, layoffs and the possibility of closure of business.

The technology start-up ecosystem in India is a bouquet of approximately 9,300 companies, employing more than 4 lakh people[1]. According to a Nasscom report of May 2020, 90 per cent of the respondent start-ups were facing revenue declines, 70 per cent had a runway of less than three months and 30–40 per cent were in the process of shutting down temporarily or permanently.[2]

Under such tough and unpredictable circumstances, when survival itself is a question, the entire venture capital has also come to a standstill. A lot of the deals that had come by in those early months of the pandemic were because of the already existing engagements. Term sheets had been taken back by venture capitalists (VCs), not just in India but globally. The reality was grim. Or was it?

There are many interesting stories where companies are pivoting their business models. Be it Yulu's partnership with Dunzo to offer cycles and e-vehicles to Dunzo's delivery boys or Bigbasket delivering through Uber. Be it Urban Company's foray into sanitization services or gamification of the Myntra platform to keep customers engaged during lockdown. And it is not just an emerging ecosystem within the start-ups but even long-term partnerships with large companies have been made; be it ITC delivering through e-commerce start-ups or innovative ventilator

---

[1] Alnoor Peermohamed, 'Covid Impact: 70% of Startups Have Cash Reserves to Last Less Than 3 Months,' *The Economic Times*, 19 May 2020, https://economictimes.indiatimes.com/small-biz/startups/newsbuzz/indias-startups-story-hanging-by-a-thread/articleshow/75817730.cms?from=mdr, last accessed on 4 December 2020.

[2] Venkatesh Ganesh, '40 Per Cent of Start-ups on the Verge of Shutting Down: Nasscom,' 19 May 2020, https://www.thehindubusinessline.com/info-tech/40-of-start-ups-on-the-verge-of-shutting-down-nasscom/article31624141.ece, last accessed on 9 December 2020.

systems coming out of this ecosystem and being produced at scale.

So, is there a silver lining? How are VCs working with their current companies and what's their message to new entrepreneurs? Is this a good time to start?

I reached out to Vivek Mansingh, General Partner at YourNest VC Fund. Vivek has had an incredibly successful global career of more than 30 years across two continents. During his career, he worked with the likes of Steve Jobs, Michael Dell and John Chambers. Vivek holds six US patents and is a post-graduate from Stanford University.

Even before I actually got to interview Vivek, I got a glimpse of his mentoring skills. His first question on our introductory call made me introspect. He asked me what was my motivation and purpose behind this book. He taught me how being clear on the purpose is half the job done. He showed me how we limit our purpose by what we think is feasible rather than what may be a tough road but would make a worthwhile investment of all our resources. These are crucial lessons for any company, especially in these times and for start-ups as they focus, survive, re-invent and innovate.

VCs are visionaries—quick to spot gold as well as rocks. A lot of them have their roots outside India. So, when the pandemic was unfolding in China, they were cognizant that this is going to soon come to their portfolio companies in India. They sent out early warning signs to their portfolio companies, strongly encouraging them to think about this as a mid- to long-term trend and brace for the impact. Even though it was hard to predict the exact nature and scale of this in India, it was important to have a business continuity plan, just in case.

'We asked our portfolio companies to imagine different scenarios and how they would react to each of those. Be it employee well-being or the impending cash crunch, the plan needed to have solutions that could be kicked-off in a week and changes that were needed in the mid to long haul. We reviewed their plans and gave feedback on where and how to invest their time and money. This was the time to re-prioritize [and to] focus on core businesses and product innovations. Any business model built on discounting was riskier than ever.'

As the lockdowns began to get extended, start-ups were impacted in more ways than one. On one hand was the liquidity challenge; on the other were issues in both the supply chain as well as demand. With the country under lockdown, B2C customers were staying indoors. Only essential services were allowed. B2B deals started getting delayed as companies began to re-evaluate their budgets. Sectors such as travel and hospitality were among the worst hit. Others such as telemedicine and e-education saw opportunity in the crisis. Redistribution of resources began to happen. VCs started coaching their start-ups to think afresh.

'I spoke to many entrepreneurs and told them that whether they have been CEOs of their start-ups for two or five years doesn't matter any more. Whatever was done in the pre-COVID era doesn't hold much ground. They need to imagine that they've just stepped into the CEO role, which means that they should take a fresh look at the business and its finance, sales, marketing, product road map, teams, etc. They need to come up with a new business plan and strategy and also re-commit emotionally to this new plan.

'Furthermore, founders should re-evaluate and analyse the value proposition of their products. A new business plan and strategy may need a new product road map. When necessities have overtaken wants and luxuries, is the product still relevant? The market and consumers are no longer enticed by wishful products because there is no money to buy those. A need-based product that is cost-effective is what the market will likely buy.

'Next, the sales focus in the short term should be skewed towards growing industries such as healthcare, financial services, education, online retail, collaboration tools, online gaming and entertainment. These are the segments that are doing well and have the wherewithal to buy. The marketing pitch and go-to-market should be charted keeping these industries in mind.

'As an example, a company I incubated, EnCloudEn, which is in the area of hybrid cloud, introduced products for work from home (WFH) and virtual office. A portfolio company of YourNest, Ka Ha Technologies, which works in the area of wearable technologies launched a few products related to management of COVID.

'Also, one may have to look at the geography of focus for sales in the short term. Founders should focus on geographies that need fewer resources and give quicker revenues. The US and Europe are reeling under serious COVID impact and economic downturn looms large there. International travel may take a while to come back. It's therefore time to focus on India, which is likely to open up faster. One of our portfolio companies had a 100 per cent focus on the US market, but now they have turned it around to have a 100 per cent India focus for the next few months.'

It's crucial to remember that although funding has thinned down, it hasn't dried up completely. VCs are cautious and eye only those start-ups that are exceptional. On 1st May, YourNest launched the SOAR programme, a pioneering fast-track funding initiative, with the single-minded objective of investing in a select few start-ups. The programme will invest anywhere between US$250,000 and US$1 million in funding—within four weeks of the application deadline, which was 14 May 2020. So how, then, can you turn around your start-up into an exceptional venture with the limited runway that you have?

'Rather than shut our doors, the VC community will embrace this uncertainty by investing in and helping grow the next generation of category creators and disruptors. Founders should not wait and watch, but act. They need to be creative, decisive, lead from the front and inspire their teams in this difficult phase. No winter lasts forever. Tough times also provide an opportunity. Companies such as Airbnb, Square and Stripe all were launched during the global financial crisis.'

Talking about how the government can help the start-up ecosystem, where on one hand, the government announced several packages for the micro, small and medium enterprise (MSME) sector and also brought start-ups under the umbrella of MSMEs, on the other hand, it decided to block the automatic route for approving foreign direct investments (FDI) from China. Vivek mentions how it is not just about solving for the credit crunch but also about making policies easier and seamless.

'The self-reliant India is an opportunity for the start-up ecosystem and many interesting start-ups will come out of it. The paperwork for starting and closing a company, if it is not successful, can be simplified further. Governments and public-sector undertakings (PSUs) should look at doing businesses with start-ups.'

There will be companies who will adapt, innovate and be nimble. However, despite best efforts of the founders, the pandemic may mean significant headcount reduction for some. Difficult decisions will be inevitable and be carried out. In such scenarios, Vivek mentors his portfolio companies to be fair, empathetic and transparent.

'If you have to let go, be upfront about it. Think like a community and provide people a few months' runway. Help them find other opportunities, wherever possible. Remember, this was the talent you took months to hire.'

While the impact of pandemic is still unfolding, venture capital is going to take a while to be where it was. While the bar for investing will be raised significantly, investors will stay amenable, adjust on the fly and look to deploy.

In getting this next set of great ideas funded during this downturn, we'll have helped create the foundation for a new set of leaders to thrive and tackle pain points in a variety of categories we so direly need to be solved in the future.

About Vivek Mansingh

Dr Vivek Mansingh is currently General Partner at YourNest, an early stage Venture Capital fund. In addition, he is Board member at Royal Orchid Hotels (Listed), Innovatia (a Canadian knowledge management company), Velocity Global (fourth fastest-growing company in US) and Janaagraha (India's leading NGO). He has incubated and invested in several start-ups.

In the past he has held leadership positions in Cisco Systems, Dell India, Portal Software Inc., Ishoni Networks, Aavid ATTI, Fujitsu and Hewlett-Packard in the US.

Vivek is an alumnus of Stanford University (Executive Business Management Programme); Queen's University, Canada (PhD in Engineering Design); and National Institute of Technology, Allahabad, (BE, Awarded Gold Medal).

Vivek holds six US patents and has published hundreds of articles and technical papers and has contributed to two books.

Dr Mansingh was listed as an honoured professional in 'National Who's Who for the United States' in the year 2000. He is the recipient of the Rotary Club's prestigious Paul Harris Fellow Award, Public Relations Council of India's highest Chanakya Innovative Leadership Award and IT Man of the Year 2016 from Enterprise Connect, US.

14

MYRESQR.LIFE

myresQR.life is India's only mobile app independent emergency alert ID that works both with and without smartphone as well as with and without the internet. This is the first-of-its-kind emergency response communication interface that bridges the gap of communication between an unidentifiable and unconscious emergency victim and the stakeholders such as family and friends, emergency care providers, ambulance services and the insurance company.

Having spent most of his life in sales, Akash Agarwal witnessed many such emergency situations either with himself or with his peers and few of these incidents resulted in the demise of the victim since information was not readily available to any stakeholder. This inspired him to find a solution which is frugal, can be used by masses and is still affordable, providing a complete end-to-end solution for an emergency victim across the globe.

With the onset of COVID-19 pandemic, myresQR.life reinvented itself to provide personal safety and hygiene products and services for the masses. For the B2B segment, myresQR.life created India's first hand sanitizer refill service and got accepted across multiple cities in India within a few weeks of launching the service. myresQR.life has also invented an intelligent sanitizer dispenser (patent pending) only for B2B customers. The smart dispenser is aimed at solving the challenges of managing, monitoring and replenishment of hand sanitizers at office premises with complete control on misuse and abuse of the facility, through internet-of-things (IoT), artificial intelligence (AI) and machine learning (ML).

∼

The best brands combine 'commerce, customer, and conscience'.

—Giles Lury

The health crisis we are all facing today is unprecedented. But so is another crisis that we do not pay much attention to: road accidents. Every year, more than 5,00,000 road accidents are reported on India's roads, claiming more than 2,00,000 lives and leaving 1,00,000 victims temporarily/permanently disabled. And yet, we do not find value in investing in an emergency response service product. We feel we are infallible.

But just like masks are our protective gear in COVID, the ability of getting a road accident victim to hospital without much delay can save a person's life. And yet, myresQR.life, a start-up in India's only medical emergency alert system, had taken time to take off. This was not the first time for Akash. His previous venture, Swasthaadhaar focused on creating digital health records, and was an idea ahead of its time.

In a time when the best of the balance sheets are in duress, a lot of young start-ups are also facing the survival question. It is in such times that I come across this unique start-up that has pivoted its business while keeping its vision of protecting lives intact. A brand that has made commercial gains out of a clear conscience and focused attention on customers' needs.

Having personally seen the journey of Akash Agarwal, founder, myresQR.life, through the lens of a friend, I have seen up close and personal the challenges of entrepreneurship. So even before the government announced lockdown and many of us started working from home, I asked Akash if he was worried about his product's relevance. Will people, who are now staying indoors, need a device that can help them in medical emergencies? Who would think about road accident safety and the importance of being able to reach the nearest hospital and automatically informing one's loved ones?

'As an entrepreneur, yes. As a human, no,' he responded.

Akash's personal experience of finding sanitizers in short supply urged him to ask a friend, who is a formulation expert, to manufacture a few bottles for his personal use. Soon after, the bottles arrived at his office.

'I observed people coming into my office. The first thing everyone was looking for was a bottle of sanitizer. People liked the product and took it home. The bottles would vanish in no time. I would reorder and the same pattern would repeat.'

Akash is an entrepreneur; someone who has a knack for opening the door when opportunity knocks. When he saw the demand and supply gap in the market, he ideated with his team if they should get into the business of sanitizers. Not only was this a business opportunity but also a way to help people in the crisis.

'People around us were finding it hard to procure sanitizers. Even the ones that were selling were overpriced. Some local brands were not even using the right formulation. On the other hand, we knew people in the supply chain whom we could trust and who could manufacture and distribute it for us. We sensed that sanitizers were here to stay. And it was better to manufacture our own product and sell under our own brand.

'We discussed if the brand should be under a new name. A mentor recommended we keep myresQR.life as the umbrella brand. We changed our tag line from "Scan to Save" to "Protecting Lives".'

The company sold 10,000 sanitizers in the first lot. Akash knew that at the scale he wanted to operate at, he would need more suppliers. He started scouting for those.

'During the crisis, several small and medium enterprises (SMEs) started to manufacture sanitizers. We, however, wanted to focus on the quality processes that were followed during the manufacturing process. So, even though the SMEs were local and could have significantly brought down our costs, we did not want to compromise on the quality of the product. People were placing their lives with the sanitizer brands. And we owed it to people to ensure that commercial gains did not precede their trust. We went in for suppliers who had [existed] for at least five years and who were Good Manufacturing Practices, World Health Organization (WHO) certified.'

During lockdown, movement of raw materials as well as the finished product was easier said than done. Akash's business partner, Naresh, was the reason the entire supply chain could be managed with minimum disruption. The company got sanitizers manufactured from far-off plants, including places such as Daman and Diu. They started selling on Amazon and through their own network and via social media marketing.

'We knew that a pure product like this wouldn't stand the test of times when big brands would come with their range of products. They had a much bigger distribution and marketing muscle. We needed to create a differentiation. Could we make a service out of this product?'

Akash started talking to people in his network about their problems with sanitizers. He learnt how corporates found pilferage to be a big problem. Organizations found it challenging to manage, monitor and replenish the hand sanitizers stationed at their multiple locations of offices and branches. He also researched how sanitizers were combustible and storing large volumes of it was a serious fire risk hazard. The team then brainstormed and leveraged their tech expertise to develop the myresQR Sanitizer Refill Services.

'Businesses were buying big cans of sanitizers and keeping them in their storage. No one was aware of the hazard of storing such a combustible material at one place. We thought of how we could handle this problem, while taking away the hassle of daily refilling.

'At the heart of the service is the Smart Dispenser traQR, which is a patent-pending AI-enabled IoT dispenser.

'The whole system is based on the two containers (the device to be refilled and the source for the refill) authenticating each other. Strict authentication avoids pilferage. Small quantity refills minimize the fire safety hazard. Built-in analytics help a business understand their usage patterns across locations. These are also used for predicting when the next refill is needed. Our service person does the refill without the business worrying about the same. The entire system is automated and takes away the hassle from the business.

'The device's IoT capabilities provide real-time information on the usage of consumables at any location, which allows for the management monitoring and replenishment of the sanitizer dispensers in a contactless manner.'

The system is currently pending a patent.

Be it malls or corporate offices, a varied landscape of customers have appreciated the product and are placing their orders for the same. Akash educates his customers about what they should look for in a good quality sanitizer and what to avoid in terms of large container storage. Even if they don't buy from him, he does this consultation in good faith.

The team at myresQR.life is a small one. It was hard to find cash. It was hard to seek funding. The team has borrowed on their credit cards, negotiated for late payments with their suppliers and borrowed from friends and family. But all this seems worthwhile as the business expands. From having the refill network in four cities, Akash has aggressive plans to expand.

'By the end of 2020, we want to have a distribution capability across all state capitals and other top five cities per state. We are hiring people across cities to be our feet on the street. We are building a central customer support system.'

Akash comes from a defence family background, and he is looking to employ 300 retired defence people to run the distribution centres across 100 cities.

He also wants to employ transgenders, acid attack victims and war widows in a scalable manner. As he candidly puts it, 'I may not have the full resources and set out to do that today. But this is my dream and I will make an honest endeavour to fulfil it.'

Akash's story is simple and yet so powerful. He did not see the crisis as a situation to mull over but as an opportunity to act. Despite being a core team of only three people, he has been able to use his network effectively to research, understand, make inroads and sell. He knows the difference between a trader and an entrepreneur. He knows how to find that unique space to be in; the importance of understanding customer's issues and providing solutions; the importance of differentiating from competitors. Post the pandemic, our administration is waking up to the importance of digital health records. Back in 2015, when Akash had focused on this need through his venture Swasthaadhaar, investors did not find the idea profitable. All this highlights the systemic pains our country needs solutions for, if it wants people to think big and innovate.

All this has taken a toll on his personal life. Knowing his family closely, I know the kind of compromises and sacrifices they made for him so that he could experiment. Akash's story has another powerful lesson; it teaches the importance of love in everyone's life. One can lead on one front if the others are well oiled.

About Akash Agarwal

Akash Agarwal is the founder of myResQR.life. He has been in the consumer retail space for more than 30 years and proudly proclaims to have started his career at the age of nine—when most kids his age were busy playing in the grounds—as an assistant to his entrepreneur mother, who was among the first few women entrepreneurs in his hometown, Agra, during the mid-1980s.

Akash completed his formal education in science and attained his post-graduate degree in management from Symbiosis Institute of International Business, followed by another post-graduate degree in economics. He has been instrumental in launching and selling multiple concept brands and products in the Indian market, from Nakshatra Diamonds, Magppie, Zwilling, Recliners India, SIGG and ZAGG to his own start-up ideas in healthcare and emergency response communication.

Akash is on a constant search for innovative ideas that can have a meaningful impact in people's daily lives. He also advises young start-ups on scaling up and on strategy for growth. He believes that there is no shortcut to hard work and success and investor funding should never be used to discount your product or services for the end consumer.

LESSON 7

BEING OPEN TO FAIL

Leadership is not only about succeeding, but also about being open to fail. Especially in times of crisis, the acceptance of failure and moving on from there to the next step and then the next is a critical leadership trait.

These are times when given the dynamicity of the situation, decisions need to be made based on the limited information available and, many a time, they need to be taken in a decentralized manner. Fail fast gets more important than learning and waiting to make the right decision. Different business models are prototyped and many of them may not work. It's OK. Leaders move on.

Crises like these cause even the strongest of businesses to falter and fail. There are times salaries are hard to come by, payments with vendors need to be re-contracted and customer refunds are impossible to make. Times like these suck and can make one feel like a failure. But it is precisely in times like these that leadership becomes critical. A wise Harvard lecturer, Tim O'Brien, once said, 'Leadership is about mobilizing others to confront and make progress on a difficult reality that they (and probably you) would rather avoid.'

There are often external circumstances beyond one's control. Be kind to yourself and your team. Re-pivot as many times as necessary. Collaborate with competitors. Leadership is not about the outcome; it is about the process. Even the decision to shut down business may look like a failure looking outwards. But the process of arriving at that decision, accepting it, communicating it and executing the failure can demonstrate leadership.

Be open to fail.

15

NAMASTAY AWAY

NamaStay Away started as an effort to make masks that create an atmosphere of positivity in times of gloom. Made from natural fabrics, with a sweat-absorbent lining, the reusable masks come in various prints and motifs. For each mask one buys from this platform, the platform donates one to the less privileged. The platform is meant to generate sustainable employment for several artisans across the country and currently employs more than 3,000 artisans from diverse demographics. Manish Tripathi's platform 'designermasks.in' not only showcases his own collection but also provides a platform for other designers to sell their products.

∼

I don't design clothes. I design dreams.

—Ralph Lauren

What comes to your mind when you think of masks? Patients? COVID? Compulsion? Have you ever associated masks with these words: fashion, style, colours? When the prime minister urged everyone to wear masks, I was one of those who felt constrained. I felt like a patient every time I stepped out wearing my blue disposable mask. It was also an added expense since the mask was not reusable. When I saw the migrant labourers on the road, I felt strange. They had no food, no employment, but they were required to procure a mask somehow. And then I came across Manish Tripathi. The fashion designer who designs for celebrities and international organizations; whose list of clients include the Board of Control for Cricket in India (BCCI) and the Prime Minister's Office; who has designed costumes for Bollywood movies, producers, directors and politicians. And yet it was not all the limelight that gave him his purpose in life. It was COVID-19.

When I first heard about Manish through a friend, I went through his Twitter handle to do some research. I was a little unsure as to how his story would fit in my book. How is he a leader? What does a fashion designer need to really lead? My presumptions about him being high-headed were put to rest when I spoke with him for the first time. My conversations with him proved me wrong. I was awed, inspired and touched by this man and his leadership, business acumen and dedication to serve the society in this time of crisis.

Manish is the creative head of two brands: AntarDesi and Naveli. While the former caters to groom wear, the latter is the bridal-wear brand. In times of COVID, when most weddings were getting postponed and people were staying home, the last thing on anyone's mind was lavish wedding couture. Business was down and uncertain. The firms employed 70 people from across different states.

'My artisans were getting anxious about their livelihood. There was no surety of when business would pick up again. Like other migrants, they too were contemplating going back to their hometowns. On the other hand, my parents, who stay in Lucknow, were asking me to come home. They were worried for my safety in Delhi. But how could I abandon my people and run away? I told my artisans to stay put. I told them we will face it all together. Like a father does not abandon his children, I felt responsible for my people. My humble beginnings gave me confidence that even if it all came down to zero, I could start from scratch,' Manish says.

Since that day, Manish's parents spoke to him several times in the day but never asked him to come home. Manish remained in touch with his workers and ensured they had enough to fend for themselves. The workers trusted him and decided to stay put. The wait was difficult and needed patience. But then came the turning point

'Days after Prime Minister Narendra Modi urged people to cover their faces when they stepped out, I went out to do my grocery shopping. What I saw there was heart-breaking. A poor man, almost in his 70s, picked up a dirty and torn mask from the road and covered his face. I went straight to my office, cut cloth and made a few masks to give to such needy people.'

Manish has not stopped since. He asked his workers if they could work from their home and make masks.

'It was a lockdown and we were not an essential service. Every morning, I would carry 50 kg of fabric on my head and sneak into my car. I would then go to each worker's house and give them the raw material. In the evening, I would collect the masks from them, sanitize and distribute these on the streets.'

Manish knew that the masks were here to stay. When he saw people in blue, white and black masks, he thought of ways to make them more colourful and vibrant.

'When I saw people in the blue, white or black masks, it seemed each was looking at the other as if they were a patient. I knew that even when the lockdown ended, masks were going to be a part of our lifestyle for a long time. I decided I would experiment with masks. I would make them a style statement, a form of self-expression.

'Just like people compliment each other on their dresses, people should also compliment each other on their masks. When one would start going to the office, the mask should be more formal. When one has to attend a party, the mask should be trendy and bright. I even started thinking of masks for brides and grooms.'

Having been in the profession of bespoke styling and designing, Manish knew each of his clients would also want masks that matched their style. Some of the corporate clients may even want their logo on the masks for their employees.

'I started experimenting with natural fabrics such as organic cotton, silk and khadi. I ideated masks for men and women. Since I had been wearing them for some time now, I knew how sweat and heat made it unbearable to wear masks. I used cotton towel fabric on the inside to solve this problem. I made quirky masks and included embroidery, prints, studs, sequins and denims.'

On 10 April 2020, Manish launched a new brand of masks, NamaStay Away.

'India has a unique culture of greeting each other. We say "namastey" to people we meet. Spelled differently, it also gives the message of staying away.'

Manish is not just selling his own masks. Rather, he launched a platform where more designers can join hands and offer their brand of designer masks. He launched an umbrella venture, an online portal, designermasks.in. All this not only gave work to his employees but also offered a ray of hope to the hand-weavers who manufactured the raw fabric. He also started selling these masks through online platforms such as Amazon.

Manish put a process in place: selling designer masks to people who could afford them and were happy to get these and using that money to manufacture and donate reusable masks to the poor and needy. On one hand, Manish was keeping his workers busy and on the other, he was happy that by distributing these masks, he was able to support the nation in its fight against COVID.

'There was something that was still amiss. I was still not able to help the last man in the queue,' says Manish.

One day, when Manish was on the road, he offered one of these free masks to a migrant who was walking on the road. The conversation with that human changed the trajectory for Manish's life. When Manish offered him the mask, the man laughed sarcastically and told him,

'I care much more for my starving family than for this mask.'

When Manish gave him something to eat, the man said,

'You are giving me today. What about tomorrow? I need work. I can beg and earn more than I made when I was working. But I was living a dignified life. My children looked up to me as a father who earned a livelihood.'

Manish knew that he needed to think out of the box. He was not happy providing someone one meal. He would rather want to provide a livelihood.

'I felt small. I wanted to teach them to fish,' shares Manish.

On one hand, the demand for designer masks was picking up and on the other, Manish was looking at how he could channelize that demand to employ more people. On his birthday, Manish took a vow to employ 50,000 people by October 2020.

Manish approached the National Small Industries Corporation and explained his plan to them. He wanted to employee women from the rural sector and offer them a way to earn their livelihood. The general manager there was very supportive. He put him in touch with the district administration of Bulandshahr, a small town in Uttar Pradesh. The administration responded with eagerness.

'I travel 200 km every day to supply the raw material to the self-help groups and train them to make the masks. They make the masks, sanitize and pack them. The next day, I collect the same and provide new raw material.'

Manish has employed more than 3,000 women. Depending on how skilled they are, they make anywhere between 25–100 masks per day.

'Several women have told me that they have never felt so liberated. Their husbands have lost a regular source of income and the income from making these masks is helping them sustain their livelihood.'

Manish is seeing all this as a stepping stone. He intends to build a network of such women, and train and employ them to produce not only masks, but also readymade garments. He is also helping them get interest-free loans to procure machinery that they can use at home.

'I am training my 70 employees to be master trainers. They are going to further train the women on making other products; right from cutting and tailoring to ironing and packaging. I am also looking at online training to scale. The road ahead is long, but the journey is worth it.'

When Manish tells me how he is also designing personal protective equipment (PPEs), along with the Indian Institute of

Technology (IIT), I am perplexed. What role does a designer have to play in a PPE?

Manish explains, 'IIT Delhi and Uflex, India's largest packaging material company, had come up with a three-layer PPE made up of a material that was both antimicrobial and antiviral. But the seams in the PPE were making these kits vulnerable to tear. I thought of ways to eliminate these seams. After spending several hours in the IIT lab and experimenting, I was finally able to help the team with a foolproof design. The design is now approved by the Defence Research and Development Organisation (DRDO) and being sent for mass production.'

As Manish puts it, 'There is a design element to everything, even a cartwheel.'

In all of this, does he not worry about his safety?

'If you follow the safety protocols, you will be safe. If you tamper with them, you and only you are responsible for the contamination. Despite all the glamour, what was missing in my life was a purpose. This work has given a new meaning to my life. I am getting only four hours of sleep every day and driving hundreds of kilometres on the road, but what keeps me going is the smiles on the women's faces, and a sense of fulfilment and gratitude.

'At each step, where I feel stuck, help and encouragement come from the most unexpected corners. The world is full of good people. That is why the world still exists. All the media attention has made me feel more responsible. I owe it to them and my people, to live up to the goals I have set for myself and my company. My bank balance may go negative, but I don't care. At this point, I want to make money so I can donate to the needy. Money is a by-product, not an end product.'

Till date, Manish has made more than 200,000 masks. A large part of the proceeds of the sale are being sent to the PM CARES fund. His work has been endorsed and admired by several media houses and eminent personalities. For Manish and the thousands of people whose lives now have a new meaning, this is just the beginning and there are miles to go.

'I am not a soldier. But I do have a machine-gun to combat the deadly virus; my sewing machine, with which I can stitch reusable cotton masks for the ones in need but cannot afford. I will continue to do my bit.'

The story of designermasks.in tells us how while no business is future proof, what wins in the end is one's commitment to society and the larger good. Everyone else comes around. Masks are a need. Manish has made them a desire.

As his four-year old niece fondly puts it, Manish is the 'maskman' the country needs, the creative lead in the long road to recovery. He is making our country 'Atmanirbhar' (self-reliant).

About Manish Tripathi

An alumnus of the prestigious National Institute of Fashion Technology (NIFT), Manish Tripathi owns the AntarDesi (designer and wedding wear for men) and Naveli (designer and wedding wear for women) labels. His brands provide customized designs to clients, which range from the BCCI to the Prime Minister's Office; from Bollywood stars to cricket and political personalities. Manish's work during the COVID-19 crisis and NamaStay Away platform has been applauded by several leaders and leading media platforms for generating employment and donating masks to the underprivileged.

16

LANDMARK

Landmark Worldwide is an international leader in the personal and professional growth, training and development industry and has had over 2.4 million people participate in its seminars, offered in more than 21 countries around the world. Landmark was founded in 1991 with a commitment to provide seminars and courses that make a profound difference to the quality of people's lives and work. Landmark began with a dynamic group of leaders, a powerful operations team and a body of intellectual properties originally developed by Werner Erhard. From its beginning in 1991 to the present day, Landmark has continued to fulfil its commitment to contribute to individuals, organizations and society. Landmark's curriculum continues to evolve, and with each refinement, Landmark elevates the quality and positive impact of its programmes.

HR.com/James McNeil recognized Landmark as one of the top leadership and development training providers in the world, in 2002. Marketdata Enterprises, Inc., which publishes the definitive report on the self-improvement industry in the United States, stated in their 2019 report that 'Landmark is recognized for having one of the best faculty bodies in the business.' Marketdata[1] *went on to report:*

Landmark's programs differ from other marketplace offerings in terms of their added depth, unique approach, and the expanded magnitude and scope of the results produced for people who participate.

The vast majority of programs in the personal growth, training and development industry rely on traditional education methods or motivational

---

[1] Marketdata Enterprises' 2019 Market Report, 'The Market For Self-Improvement Products and Services,' October 2019, 12th Edition.

techniques and theory. Traditional education's central focus is on increasing peoples' knowledge or understanding, i.e., expanding knowing. Academia refers to this as epistemologically-based education.

In contrast, Landmark's programs are about being, and Landmark is the sole program provider of ontological transformation. Ontology is the study of being and Landmark's programs include a deep look into the already-existing nature of being human, and beyond that, what is possible in being human. Landmark is a worldwide leader in the personal growth, training and development industry; and Landmark's ideas, delivery and intellectual property are unique within both the industry and society.

Landmark's programs allow participants to become aware of the underlying assumptions, beliefs and interpretations that constitute the way they view their life and the world in which they live—all of which influences and impacts their actions.

The result is a transformation in being—a breakthrough that results in immediate, lasting and dramatic shifts in people's effectiveness and quality of life.

∽

When written in Chinese, the word 'crisis' is composed of two characters. One represents danger and the other represents opportunity.

—John F. Kennedy

Seven years ago I did a transformational course, the Landmark Forum. I had heard a lot about it from people I trusted, but it took me years to finally enrol myself in the programme. Seven years later, I still feel the energy I experienced in the classroom. Every inch of my mindset was transformed in that three-day course. So powerful was the experience that I have been a proponent of that programme to anyone and everyone! The experience of a safe space for conversations; listening to others pour their hearts out; seeing lives touched and moved created a new world of possibilities.

A couple of days into the lockdown, I received an email from Landmark. Landmark was creating opportunities for its graduates (people who have done the Forum) to be in communication with the Landmark Forum Leaders, the trainers who deliver these in-person programmes. Anyone who has done the programme knows that magic gets created in the Landmark classrooms. Conversations happen and these open up one's view of the world. I was very doubtful of how the in-person communication experience of sharing could be created virtually. But knowing Landmark, I knew it was possible. How was this journey of a physical classroom to a virtual classroom for the organization? What were the challenges Landmark was helping its graduates lead their way to? And how were they different from the pre-pandemic times? I joined one of the sessions, only to be moved again by the commitment of the Forum Leaders to help their graduates deal with whatever was happening in their lives.

A week later, I was introduced to Gopal Rao, Managing Director of India operations at Landmark, by a friend's friend. On my first call with him, I asked Gopal how he would explain the concept of Landmark education to my readers.

'Consider a butter chicken curry. For a non-vegetarian person, the dish is the first thing they would order in a restaurant. There are others who are vegetarian but are OK with someone else across the table sitting and eating butter chicken. And then there are animal lovers whose first reaction on seeing the dish would be different since an animal/ bird got killed. The same dish can evoke so many reactions.

'In life too, it is not the situation that matters, but rather one's perspective (view) that can empower or disempower one's ability to lead in the situation. Landmark is all about opening up that perspective and leaving the participants in full control of their journeys. Like cricket, every ball needs a different batting stroke. In life too, one needs as many batting strokes as possible in one's armour. Landmark equips you with that,' Gopal responded.

Since its inception, Landmark Forums for new graduates usually run from Friday to Sunday and have an evening session on Tuesday. Landmark holds seminars in approximately 115 locations in more than 21 countries. It was at its Korea and Singapore offices that this pandemic was first seen as a disruptor. Governments and authorities across the globe were taking different routes and there were restrictions being announced everywhere.

'Every Forum session is attended by 150–250 people in the classroom. The situation on the ground was changing very fast. We were hearing how having gatherings was not safe any more. As cities in India began to report COVID cases, we decided to halt the physical classroom sessions for our India operations. The situation evolved so fast that we needed to do this for even our ongoing programmes. On Sunday night, we announced the same to our participants. This was the first time in the history of the programme that an ongoing course was paused,' Gopal tells me.

For a programme that has been conducted in-person for close to three decades, the natural thought was not of doing the courses online, but of temporarily pausing and consciously thinking of the next steps.

As Gopal shares, 'Historically, our programmes have been delivered in person. This allows our leaders to be present to eye contact, hand gestures, voice modulation and so forth. The obvious question was: can this be available virtually? While we thought it would work to some degree, both our leaders and students were surprised and greatly satisfied by the degree of efficacy that was achieved, and the real-life results that were delivered, via an online delivery.

'We're sure the reason behind this is that Landmark's unique methodology works in conversation, regardless of the medium.'

Landmark began designing a communication module that helped them be in touch with the existing graduates. People who had already attended the Forum would be enthusiastic to participate in the digital programmes. This would also help the Forum Leaders settle into the digital mode of delivering, and the learnings from this experience could then be used to think about further scaling the digital coaching.

'Our Forum Leaders did not just need help with learning technology tools to be able to control more than 100–200 people virtually, they also needed to be trained on other aspects. Our Forum Leaders were used to looking at the participants and moving around the classroom. Here they were staring at their screens. They could not move around. Their home internet connection had to work well. They needed to be fully present despite the household chores and the presence of kids and family members around them in their own homes. They needed to be dressed well when conducting these programmes. And well prepared for all the exigencies that could happen. Suddenly there could be a participant who could unmute and start talking out of turn. Or a participant who switched on their video inadvertently. All of that needed to be handled appropriately.'

In a physical class, a teacher can see who is drifting off and bring that person back into the discussion in the classroom. It is hard to do that on a digital medium. The Forum Leaders need to not only put double the effort in retaining people's attention but also be comfortable with the fact that some of the participants may have just dozed off or gone to make their tea or coffee. Unlike a physical classroom, having two-way conversations while still keeping the rest of the class engaged is tough. How do you replicate the breakout sessions where a group of participants talk to each other and open up?

There were also challenges for the participants. They were no longer in a safe space but inside their homes and with people around them. Unlike a physical world where the participants met each other during those three days and formed a human connection, the same was not feasible on the digital medium.

'We could get stuck with all the above issues and do nothing about them. But we decided to shift our perspectives. And just by opening up to newer ways of operating and keeping our commitment to empowering the participants in achieving what was important in their individual lives, no matter what, solutions began to emerge. That context made it easier. The leaders committed to offering a compelling value proposition to the participants, such that they don't need to demand the participants' attention but rather the same would be forthcoming.'

The Forum decided to focus on the millions of its existing graduates and work with them to begin with. The idea was to learn and adapt, while empowering this set of already enrolled people. Landmark launched new programmes for the graduates which were tailored to the current times. They also recognized how longer programmes were less effective digitally, especially as screen fatigue sets in. The organization launched shorter modules of learning.

A Place to Stand: Dealing with Challenging, Disruptive and Uncertain Times was launched in April. The intention of this two-hour programme was to empower people in dealing with the disruptive and uncertain times.

'We decided to work with our existing graduates, making sure we are there for them in these times. We wanted to leave them ready and stronger to face these situations. We heard people being worried about job losses to being stuck at home with unsupportive partners. Under all these circumstances, our role was to provide people the right tools to be able to see new perspectives in that situation. As humans, we are not used to uncertainty. No one likes uncertainty. Right from where we keep our home keys to the predictability of living, we saw our graduates baffled by the quick change of their external worlds. While we could not alter the external world, we could alter our view of it. We could make our graduates feel in control and then take actions knowing that all is not lost,' Gopal shares.

A series of other programmes have been launched since then and many more are in the pipeline. *Being with a Landmark Forum Leader: Opening up Communication, Freedom, Power and Choice* offers a platform to open up about issues one is dealing with.

'Earlier people could walk into our centres and access the leaders. This virtual programme replicates that experience and creates access for graduates to communicate with the leaders.'

At times like this, often people are just trying to survive and they forget the importance of having their lives make a difference even when things are difficult. A new course *Self-Expression: Now More Than Ever* has been recently launched with the objective of helping people express themselves authentically.

In all of this, Gopal sees how people are actually becoming conscious of what really matters in their lives, including appreciating the people who are in their lives. People are realizing how personal relationships matter much more than anything else and are reaching out to Forum Leaders as they set out in creating a new future, accepting themselves and others the way they are.

'We will continue to develop and offer programmes that make a profound difference to human possibilities. In terms of how we deliver those programmes, while we remain committed to the power and human connection available in our in-person programmes, I'm sure we will continue to leverage technology and offer online programmes. Our leaders want to meet the participants, feel their stories, hold their hands and see the unsaid. We have people from 20 to 60 years of age in our classrooms and this diverse group coming together learns a lot just by being in the same room for three days; without interruptions and in a safe space. As they say, "necessity is the mother of invention," and the current conditions spurred us to create a process that, in normal times, would have easily taken several months, if not years.'

For an organization that went from 30 years of offering in-person programmes to delivering more than 100 courses online in less than 60 days, the story of Landmark tells how commitment to one's customer's needs and finding ways to deliver on those are the hallmark of a great institution. Unlike school or college education, transformative education is not an education one would worry much if it were not available. However, the need of such an education is much more today than ever and instead of being stuck in one way of being, organizations such as Landmark are prioritizing what value they can bring to their graduates. Cheers to the unexpected levels of impact and contribution these online programmes are creating in the participants' lives.

About Gopal Rao

Gopal Rao is a senior programme leader at Landmark Worldwide. He has over 25 years of experience and expertise in delivering programmes to groups and individuals and has conducted courses for over 200,000 people across the globe. As Managing Director, India and Operations Manager at Landmark Education, Gopal heads the organization's India operations. Under his able leadership, Landmark has had over 83 per cent cumulative annual growth (CAG) in the last 15 years.

Gopal has special expertise working with large groups to achieve highly effective and breakthrough results for individuals in areas critical to their quality of life: productivity, confidence, communication, handling difficult challenges and, most critically, in the area of relationships.

Prior to joining Landmark, Gopal held the position of Group Product Manager in Johnson and Johnson (Pharmaceuticals).

Gopal Rao is an MBA with a degree in pharmacy from Mumbai University. He is an avid reader, flautist, collector of curios, and loves dogs and cats.

LESSON 8

INNOVATION

Many of us are familiar with stories about how American infantry kept trucks and jeeps rolling during World War II, even when spare parts weren't available. Used to tinkering with jalopies in their garages, the young soldiers were able to jury-rig fixes with whatever materials were on hand.

In response to the coronavirus pandemic, innovators are jumping in to help. Around the world, beer-makers and distilleries have shifted production to hand sanitizers. In Italy, a start-up engineering company began quickly using 3D printers to create the valves used in ventilators. Those just-in-time valves are saving lives.

The current crisis is bringing a whole new set of innovations. Sectors such as medicine, education and industrial plant set-ups are all going digital. Google and Apple are collaborating on contact tracing. Dunzo is working with brands to get the products delivered at one's doorstep. Yulu, in turn, is partnering with Dunzo to provide bikes to Dunzo's partners. ITC's personal care team deserves recognition for introducing a range of new healthcare and hygiene products for households. Its hospitality team curated a gourmet menu, which recreates the ITC dining experience for their customers in the comfort of their homes. While these are just a few examples, leaders across industries continue to strive to change and innovate to ensure that they deliver nothing short of excellence in their products and services to their customers, despite the pandemic.

It is said that innovation and creativity love crises and constraints. Crisis brings out constraints and makes innovation almost a forcing function. Leaders often leverage consultants to get a fresh, outside perspective on their organizations to find opportunities to innovate. A crisis can have much the same effect, putting the spotlight on vulnerabilities and problem areas, great and small, which we've been ignoring or are just plain unaware of. When a crisis hits, we are forced to confront the truth about how our systems work (or don't). How things can be done better or more efficiently becomes glaringly obvious. All of a sudden, opportunities for innovation are staring us in the face.

During a crisis, customer needs also undergo a sea change. Innovation is about the simple adaptations to those needs. If customers are scared to eat out, takeaway is an innovation. Similarly, contactless delivery is an innovation, as are metal disinfectants and workplace redesign. Changing plant operations to ensure social distancing without compromising on the output is again an innovation. Pivoting from selling to renting business models is an innovation. Finding alternate supply partners, if the others are locked down or shut down temporarily, is also an innovation.

Venture capitalists I spoke to told me how despite the cash crunch, this is the best time to fund innovations. In good times, no one wants to de-risk a sailing boat, but when the storm is strong and the winds are against the tide, innovation is the only option. And leaders see it as an opportunity, rather than just a means of survival.

17

CAFE DELHI HEIGHTS

Cafe Delhi Heights is a place that truly celebrates the Saddi Dilli spirit. Just like the city, the cafe offers big-hearted portions of deliciously cooked dishes.

The inspiration behind Cafe Delhi Heights was a place where a whole family can dine together. It is a place for all generations; the young find it a 'happening' place while the elderly find it comfortable. The interiors of Cafe Delhi Heights is a beautiful amalgamation of various designs and seating arrangements. From low seating to chill and unwind with your gang to booth seating with LCDs for a cosy dine out with your special ones, from community tables to the bohemian-style cafe lounge for casual moments, Cafe Delhi Heights offers something for each of its patrons.

Their menu features dishes from every corner of the planet, depicting the true cosmopolitan spirit of Delhi. One can savour every kind of cuisine, in the form of a hearty breakfast or a mouth-watering lunch or a lavish dinner. They have scrumptious appetizers as well as delectable desserts, and each of their dishes reflects their personal twist and the best of flavours.

Spreading its wings over 24 outlets, Cafe Delhi Heights has outlets in Delhi and NCR, Mumbai, Pune and Chandigarh.

∽

One cannot think well, love well, sleep well, if one has not dined well.

—Virginia Woolf

What are your weekend plans?

Umm…cooking, doing the dishes and then some more cooking.

It seems like ages when weekend plans were about going to a nearby restaurant for an experience. Much of monday lunch conversations at the office were about the restaurant one visited over the weekend and the best dish on the menu. My mother had been planning a surprise party for us on our first wedding anniversary in April. She was going to invite our friends and family to a nearby restaurant. Eventually, my husband and I celebrated our first anniversary cooking and doing the dishes. Like ours, several other birthdays, anniversaries and special occasions moved away from exotic Michelin restaurants to our own kitchens. Ever since restaurants shut due to the lockdown that began in March, weekends and celebrations have not been the same again.

Even when Lockdown 5.0 was in the making, restaurants were required to remain shut. An industry whose market value is estimated to be ₹4 trillion[1] and that employs more than 7 million people was completely shut. It was clear that even when the lockdown ended and the government allowed restaurants to operate, it would take months before people actually started feeling safe enough to dine out. Estimates put together by CRISIL Research, earlier this month, suggested India's organized dine-in restaurants are likely to register a 40–50 per cent drop in revenue this fiscal.[2]

As I connect with Vikrant Batra, owner of Cafe Delhi Heights, to understand how he is thinking, I half expect a dejected business leader telling me all is lost. For what is a business supposed to do when they cannot open. But Vikrant is a positive leader and he tells me that he strongly believes that this too shall pass. He tells me that the industry needs a lot more collaboration with the aggregators, mall owners and the government.

---

[1] 'Market Value of Restaurants and Food Service Industry in India in Financial Year 2019, by Segment,' *Statista*, https://www.statista.com/statistics/1112822/india-value-of-restaurants-and-food-service-industry-by-segment/, last accessed on 5 December 2020.

[2] 'Covid-19 to Eat up half of restaurant revenue this Fiscal,' CRISIL, https://www.crisil.com/en/home/newsroom/press-releases/2020/05/covid-19-to-eat-up-half-of-restaurant-revenue-this-fiscal.html, last accessed on 5 December 2020.

Of Cafe Delhi Heights's 24 self-owned outlets across Gurgaon, Delhi, Noida, Chandigarh, Pune and Maharashtra, 90 per cent are in malls. It also operates two outlets in the Delhi airport, one each in the domestic and international terminals. The chain has been awarded the prestigious Times Food and Nightlife Awards 2020 for being the most popular casual dining restaurant.

On 14 March, Vikrant was preparing to open a new outlet under a new umbrella brand in Dwarka, a posh locality of Delhi. On 15 March, the Government of Maharashtra passed a directive and four of his outlets were shut down with immediate effect.

'Before the pandemic, I woke up every day reviewing the sales numbers of the different outlets. In the initial few days as this was unfolding, I felt this was another of those SARS and Ebola, which will pass without impacting India in a big way. I have been in the restaurant business for close to 30 years and have been witness to many major events. But we had never shut down for a long period. So that thought did not occur to me,' says Vikrant.

'But as the numbers rose in Maharashtra, the chief minister passed an order to shut the restaurants till 31 March. On 15 March, a new outlet was added in this daily reporting, but the very next morning was very different. Overnight, the sales of four outlets went down to zero. It was quite disconcerting and took a while for the feeling to sink in. I reside in Delhi and since this was happening in the far-away outlets, it troubled me even more. I was not there physically with my staff as this was unfolding,' Vikrant adds.

This was soon followed by the Delhi government passing a similar order. By 19 March, the business had come to a complete standstill.

'Even before the formal shutdown in Delhi/NCR, our footfalls had become almost negligible. Crowds were getting scarce and sales were on a decline. Our staff was also under tremendous stress. We could have continued takeaways. But we wanted to step back and prioritize our staff's safety. We allowed the staff to go back to their hometowns, if they wished to. For those who stayed back, we opened up our corporate office premises and asked them to stay there.'

A restaurant's operations, especially if it is a chain that employs a thousand people, are not just about the kitchen, but also entails planning for the inventory, compliance with regulations, marketing, finance, logistics, IT, interior planners, menu team, human resource and so on. There was communication done for each of these departments to plan for a no-operation situation for the next month.

'The compliance department kept a keen eye on the state and central government directives. The inventory department ensured that all the perishables were consumed or distributed, the rest of the inventory carefully reserved and future orders put on hold. The marketing team held the front of customer engagement, so that customers knew we were closed and were engaged in our social messages. Be it sharing some of our recipes online or spreading the message of social distancing, our social media handles became more active. The logistics team started planning for online deliveries. All this while none of these people had ever worked from home. Everyone was learning and adapting,' Vikrant shares with me.

The manager of each of the outlets was keeping in touch with the staff, constantly checking if they needed support or were stuck anywhere. The team was lucky that most of their staff could reach their hometowns before the trains and public transport were brought to a halt.

'There were different WhatsApp groups over which we continued to remain in touch at various levels.'

While on one end, the chain paid the rent and salaries for March, they were unsure whether they'd still be in a position to do so if the pandemic continued.

Cafe Delhi Heights is about an experience. It is more than just good food. Known for its ambience, it was hard to replicate that experience virtually or through online mode of delivery.

But survival was the need of the hour.

'We used the initial days of the lockdown to identify the dishes best suited for takeaways. Our remaining staff could prepare these dishes, as the ingredients for these were not hard to procure and were safe. We trained our staff on the World Health Organization (WHO) safety protocols. We trimmed down a menu of 250 dishes to 35 dishes, which we began to deliver through online aggregators. This helped us recover some of our fixed expenses,' Vikrant shares with me how the business adapted to the 'new normal'.

As Vikrant was dealing with what was happening at his own organization, he also saw the effects of the pandemic across the industry. Being a part of the management committee of the National Restaurant Association of India (NRAI), he saw the enormity of the problem. While NRAI supported the need of the lockdown and prioritizing lives over livelihood, its members were facing an existential crisis.

'NRAI has been a closely knit body. Just as the issue of commissions with the online aggregators had settled in, the body had a bigger task at hand. How long was this going to last? How do we pay our rents and salaries?' says Vikrant.

It is easy to ask the mall owners to waive off the rents. But who pays for their costs then? It is easy to ask restaurants to pay their staff. But who will bear that cost when revenue is zero?

NRAI began engaging with the government at various levels. It requested unemployment pay support through the Employees' State Insurance Corporation (ESIC), Ministry of Labour and Employment. Out of approximately 3.20 crore beneficiaries of the ESIC scheme, over 50 lakh belong to the hospitality sector. NRAI also asked for urgent working capital support at the lowest possible interest, as close to the repo rate. A proposal to allow the restaurant industry to avail Input Tax Credit (ITC) on GST was also tabled. They also requested all pending tax refunds to be expedited. Last, but not the least, an urgent need to create a fair and equitable e-commerce policy for the sector was felt.

'For a businessman, it is not easy to let go of your people or furlough them. In the service industry, our staff is our biggest asset. We know our staff by their names. But people need to understand that no one likes to suddenly cut salaries, if they can still afford to pay. We need to give them the confidence that we are not abandoning them and that we are trying to tide this over together,' Vikrant puts it candidly.

Rough industry estimates peg daily losses in the organized sector of the industry to be around ₹200 crore. A three-month shut down was expected to bleed the industry by close to ₹20 thousand crore.

As Vikrant and the NRAI team were gearing up for the future, they were thinking out of the box. NRAI launched a platform named Rise for Restaurants, to support its members and their employees.

'Diners can support restaurants by buying virtual cash worth ₹1,000 at a flat 25 per cent discount today from an expansive list of restaurants across India on the platform's website, and redeem it in the future against dining bills at the respective restaurants. At the time of purchase, customers pay only ₹250. This amount will contribute towards paying the wages and salaries of restaurant employees. The remaining ₹500 is to be paid by the customer only when they dine at the restaurant.'

The virtual cash can be used within six months from the purchase date, with limitless purchases and no minimum expenditure amount, blackout dates or redemption conditions. This move ensures revenue for the immediate survival of the restaurant's employees and it attracts patrons to dine out at a discount in the near future.

Cafe Delhi Heights has also partnered with NRAI's 'Feed The Needy' initiative.

'We have contributed in cash, while some of the other restaurants in the association have worked to prepare and distribute food. As of 30 May, we have served food to close to 1 crore people. The body coordinated with local authorities and NGOs to assess the demand. Member restaurants cooking food sought permission under essential services. Members distributing food sought movement passes.'

Cafe Delhi Heights began its operations on 1 June 2011. Exactly nine years later, as I chat with Vikrant, he is ready to start again.

Sitting in one of his outlets and ensuring that the outlet is sanitized and prepared to open up for takeaways, it is a new beginning.

'I am at my Janakpuri outlet. It feels like my first day at Cafe Delhi Heights. I am personally auditing the sanitization and the safety protocols. We need to rework on our sitting arrangements, make our customer processes touchless and redesign the menus. My staff is under distress and just my presence here motivates them. It is a fresh start,' Vikrant shares with me.

While several restaurants are shutting down and some are re-pivoting to newer business models such as delivering groceries, Vikrant is hopeful that things will soon be better.

'We are social animals. We love to meet. Food is a religion in India and special occasions are incomplete without dining. Even in the lockdown, the highest sharing on the social platforms is happening over food. Food is a conversation-starter, a great way to build relationships. Chefs across the world are building brand recall and loyalty by sharing recipes and hosting cooking sessions.

'People are indoors because of the lockdown. I am confident that with the necessary arrangements, people will return. 2020 is going to be about survival,' says Vikrant.

Vikram too is thinking of diversifying into B2B supplies to others in the food industry.

'With the reduced staff, not everyone will want to bake their own breads or make their own sauces. It is an area we are actively exploring.'

Already bleeding under high supply costs, missing labour and low demand, discounts are going to vanish.

As Vikrant puts it, 'Our sector will likely be among the last few to get permissions to fully operate. Dine-ins will take a long time to be allowed. Even when we get permissions, a lot needs to change in our supply chain, kitchen operations and interiors to ensure social distancing. The cost of operations is expected to increase while the demand will take a while to come back to pre-COVID days.'

In all this, there is a silver lining. At a personal level, Vikrant tells me how this pandemic will help the younger generation become more grounded.

'Future generations are seeing how things can overturn in a few weeks. It will build resilience in them and they will learn not to take things for granted, even when their fathers and grandfathers are in thriving businesses,' says Vikrant.

It was—and continues to be—every restaurant owner's nightmare to have their staff or customers get infected while dining. While takeaway chains such as Domino's continued operations during the lockdown and while our quick-service restaurants can bounce back quicker, the road to recovery will be longer for places such as Cafe Delhi Heights. The industry is staring at a recession where close to 30 per cent of the staff may be left unemployed forever.

'Hard choices, support from the highest levels and innovation can help minimize the effects of these damages,' Vikrant puts it succinctly.

About Vikrant Batra

Vikrant Batra is a trendsetter in the restaurant industry. Food has always been the forte and the key feature of his brands. He believes in not only understanding the palette of the audience but also innovating and experimenting with it in the most comfortable manner.

A graduate from Hindu College, University of Delhi, Vikrant did a restaurant management course from the University of California. He earned his MBA degree from FORE School of Management, Delhi. He started his career working at Batra Banquets, a business he inherited, and later went on to envision and set up Cafe Delhi Heights.

With a vision to establish a fine-dining space with an affinity towards art, Vikrant's other contributions to the capital's restaurants include Nueva Dining and Bar and Dhansoo Cafe.

Vikrant Batra is the winner of many prestigious awards such as the Restaurant Entrepreneur of the Year 2018 awarded by the Federation of Hotel & Restaurant Associations of India (FHRAI),

Restaurateur of the Year: North Region award at the Indian Restaurant Awards 2017, Restauranteur of the Year 2019 by Food Food Awards and many more.

18

360 REALTORS

360 Realtors is one of the largest tech-enabled Institutional Channel Partners (ICPs) in India. From a humble beginning in 2014, the company has facilitated transactions worth ₹8,550 crore so far. It helps buyers throughout the property purchase cycle, right from property search to the transaction to the post-purchase support. Currently, it operates out of 42 offices with a total workforce of around 1,200. Around 80 per cent of the revenue comes from primary residential sales. In recent times, the company has made successful forays into complementary business verticals such as strategic advisory, real estate media, home loans and real estate franchises alongside leasing and sale of commercial assets.

~

There is nothing like staying at home for real comfort.

—Jane Austen

In the world that is staring at major job losses and where more and more organizations are contemplating remote working culture as the new norm, who would be thinking of buying office spaces or residential homes? I assume no one. This makes me curious about how the real estate industry is dealing with this pandemic. Prior to this pandemic, the real estate industry was adjusting to various structural changes and other reforms introduced by the government. The collapse of the Infrastructure Leasing & Financial Services (IL&FS) had crunched the liquidity in the sector. Goods and services tax (GST) reforms were beginning to stabilize. Lower rates on home loans were helping and the demand was beginning to boost up. It was projected that the real estate industry will contribute to 13 per cent of the gross domestic product (GDP) by the year 2025. However, COVID has thrown all projections out of the window. After all, who is thinking of real estate investment? Who wants a bigger office space? How can one even think of buying real estate without a physical site visit, which is impossible in the current situation? And will the labour ever come back? What about the closed factories that have brought the supply of raw materials to a grinding halt?

I reach out to Ankit Kansal, founder and managing director, 360 Realtors, a real estate advisory firm that operates both in the residential and commercial space. Eighty per cent of the firm's business comes from residential real estate. The company operates out of 42 cities, employs 1,200 people, works with 680 developers and has handled close to 6,000 projects. In just six years of its operations, they have facilitated transactions worth ₹8,550 crore. 360 Realtors deals in primary buying and does not engage in re-selling of any kind.

The first realizations of the pandemic for Ankit, however, came from his other business, Indsource International, which is a buying house and a liasioning company for imports and exports.

'Many of the employees of Indsource were placed out of India. When China started reporting COVID cases, our staff stationed in China returned to India. From across the globe, we started calling our Indian staff back home.'

Ankit did not yet anticipate the crisis coming to India. When COVID cases saw an uptick, he began to prepare his staff for work-for-home mode.

'We are a high touchpoint, offline business. Our sales executives form our backbone. They build long-term relationships with the customer and gain the customer's trust over a number of meetings. It is this trust and relationship that finally facilitate a deal. More than the cost, it is an experience consideration for the customer. Sixty per cent of our staff is into customer/client-facing work. Most of them operate over phone calls, physical meetings, paper brochures and in-person discussions. While it may seem naive, most did not know what Zoom was or any other digital meeting tool for that matter.'

When Ankit first told them that they would need to work from home, virtually meet their customers and be trained to close deals without meeting their clients, the first reactions were of disbelief and resignation. After all, how could we expect someone who was putting in their lifetime's income into this one deal to do all of that virtually?

'Closing the deal was a secondary goal. The primary goal was to get the staff accustomed to the virtual infrastructure and make sure each sales person was doing at least two virtual meetings a day.'

Some of the executives reported a backlash from customers who felt that the company was being too aggressive in pushing the transaction. While the business did see customers being jittery and losing interest completely, Ankit's staff also reported that the clients were now getting more time at home and wanted to use this break to plan their real estate investment.

'Thanks to the work-from-home situation, people have time to listen to our sales executives. It was the time to think beyond transactions, time to build relationships over continuous engagements.'

Just as Ankit needed an alternative to the physical meeting, he knew the business also needed an alternative to a physical site visit. His team started reaching out to major real estate developers who were also navigating the same situation. Developers, aggregators and advisory firms started investing in technology to give the customer an experience of a virtual site visit, while sitting in the safety of their homes.

'Detailed yearly plans of making everything digital in the multiple sectors has been in the pipeline, since the government envisioned creating a Digital India. Nobody could have ever imagined that a pandemic such as COVID would accelerate this process up to its optimum and make digital presence a matter of sustenance for all the businesses around. Similar kind of developments happened for the realty sector as well. With homebuyers stuck in their homes for an extended period of almost 50 plus days, developers and realty portals reformed and modified their online presence to reach out to their customer base and gain maximum traction.

'One of the most popular mediums has been webinars. Buyers are interested in listening to the experts' point of view and raising several questions; this trend reflects their genuine interest in considering realty as an avenue for investment. Today, a regular income-earning individual closely studies the market trends, and looks for alternatives to maximize their savings. With the market being so topsy-turvy, real estate has evolved to be a promising avenue.

'The lockdown period has also made developers realize how advanced technologies such as Augmented Reality and Virtual Reality are needed to satiate the expectations of the homebuyers sitting at their homes wanting to see the exact replica of their future homes. Their keenness to introduce them in their business is also linked to the fact that they want to step ahead of their competition by providing a unique engagement experience to their prospective customers.

'Virtual events could be the next evolution in how properties can be marketed, promoted and sold digitally. Very shortly, 360 Realtors would be conducting its flagship event Prop Show virtually as E-Prop Show. The event will showcase numerous projects from various developers in one window. It's going to be a very unique gamified experience, where a customer can do everything which happens in an offline exhibition while staying in the safety and comfort of one's home. This virtual show will forever redefine the exhibition space,' Ankit tells me, sharing the company's plans.

Technology was one aspect. The other aspect was making our sales people believe in it.

'Despite investments in training, technology and employee engagement, there were people who just could not cope with this new environment and took a conscious career break. There were also people whose intentions were in the right place, but they were struggling. Living in crowded homes with background noise, they were finding it difficult to take formal customer calls. We tried to train them on other workstreams which needed less facetime with customers. This cross training helped us do a healthy reallocation of our work, with minimal impact on either the employees or productivity.'

Customers are adapting to the new normal of virtual meetings and e-site visits. The month of May reported 60 per cent of the planned turnover. Sale deals worth ₹200 crore were signed.

'Some of these are deals with clients with whom we have had a long-standing relationship. When you hear about us from someone who has already transacted through us, you trust us more and are more realistic,' Ankit tells me.

Ankit shares interesting anecdotes of customers who are now looking to build a house in Goa as their second home.

'One of our customers said he wanted a back-up home in Goa. Should COVID strike again, he would rather be on a beach than in a crowded place.'

There are also some customers who want to buy a bigger house as they work from home.

'People want homes with a separate working area and where their meetings are not constantly interrupted by the sounds from the kitchen.'

On one hand, the other investment options are becoming volatile and real estate is being seen as a long-term winner; on the other hand, liquidity, supply and labour issues are already leading to project delays. On one hand, home loans are getting cheaper; on the other hand, jobs are becoming less stable and people are worried about their financial futures. What has this meant for a company like 360 Realtors?

'We are acting as a bridge between customers and developers, taking each other's pain point to them. We voiced our customers' concerns and worked with developers to innovate on their payment offerings. Several developers are now offering insurances at little to no extra cost. Should you lose your job, you don't need to pay your EMI. You can pay now and change your mind in six months. Builders are also offering price guarantees should the prices drop. Book now with a small amount and pay later has seen a rise in adoption.'

The builders are, on the other hand, working with the regulators and the government to solve the liquidity crisis. Not having access to capital is the biggest hurdle to timely completion of the projects. Migration of labour and operating factories with the appropriate safety protocols are only going to push their costs of operation higher. Add to that the slump in demand, making it infeasible to pass these costs to the customers.

Labour is the other major pain point for the labour-intensive sector. Most of the labour has gone to their hometowns. With no end in sight to the crisis, they are not expected to come back any time soon.

'Stopping construction work abruptly caused the biggest churn in the migrant labourers' livelihoods. We either revise their wages and make them more attractive, or wait for them to come back organically. Each builder with its own pockets is evaluating its options. There are active considerations, for example, to pay for the commute of these labourers when they decide to return.'

The government is constantly working with the bodies and bringing in the much-needed changes.

'Till now, GST used to be imposed as soon as the invoice was generated. In several sectors, the actual payment is delayed to some extent, which means GST has to be paid before the payment in that case. The government is considering a cash-based system, where one can pay GST after receiving the cash. This would ensure that the real estate developers do not have to pay GST from their own capital.

'The repo rate cut in late May, along with the move of extending loan moratorium for another six months will be extremely helpful in lowering the financial stress.

'I also laud the government's infusion package of ₹30,000 crore for non-banking financial companies (NBFCs) and giving six months' Real Estate [Regulation and Development] Act (RERA) extension to developers under the natural route, which is also a welcome step as it will give developers some relief and help them complete their projects on time.'

There is also a need to lower the stamp duty, registration fees and other similar charges. Simplifying the formalities would also be a major help. Instead of having to go through multiple processes that require many approvals, an online single-window purchase is the need of the hour.

Switching gears and talking about commercial real estate, Ankit mentions that this is a year to focus on survival. A large part of the workforce is likely to work from home through the rest of 2020 and early 2021. The remote working culture will mean that companies require lesser spaces. Talking about the re-designing of office spaces, Ankit throws light on how more spaces would be open, floor plans will be de-densified and provisions made for cross ventilation of fresh air instead of air conditioners. Sophisticated air filters will be in-built.

'An entire new gamut of services will emerge, creating newer workstreams for the real estate developers. Social distancing would mean that companies can house a lesser number of people within the same area. Even within our office, we have removed some desks already. Open offices will be converted into rooms with boundaries.

'We have seen large commercial deals being temporarily put on hold. Companies are reconsidering those investments. Many organizations will ask for rental concessions as well. Generally, office rentals constitute 5–9 per cent of the topline. As regular businesses have disrupted in many organizations, they will try to revisit their agreement and ask for some concession. Some companies have reached out to us with a different location in Tier-II. Reverse migration is here to stay.'

Is there a road to recovery? I ask Ankit for his thoughts on this.

'This pandemic has given birth to an anti-China sentiment. Global conglomerates will try to shift their supply chain out of China. India can be a viable alternative. The prime minister's push for being self-dependent, *Aatma Nirbhar*, will lead to more commercial activity. We are already seeing companies considering bigger warehouses.

E-commerce is booming and the demand for their warehouse space is consistently peaking. If India can convert this into an opportunity to become an export superpower, commercial real estate will bounce back in no time,' says Ankit.

Ankit also talks of another silver lining that comes through investments from non-resident Indians (NRIs).

'NRIs pay in dollars and the recent fall in rupee against the US dollar has led to lower price for them. At this time, the projects by reputed developers that are attractively priced will get NRI attention, as they will see good appreciation in the mid- to long-term. NRIs are seeing this as a great opportunity to secure their lifestyles in India. They are also investing in commercial spaces, expecting to make good gains in the mid-term.'

As a leader, Ankit is carefully treading the lines of what is best for the company and its stakeholders—be it employees, developers or end customers. Digital upgradation will be paving the path for the new normal, as post COVID, people will continue to be apprehensive of physical meetings. Players missing on the dynamism of integrating traditional and advanced practices will be at a loss.

About Ankit Kansal

Ankit Kansal is the managing director and chief executive officer (CEO) of 360 Realtors. He is a visionary serial entrepreneur who has built a host of successful businesses from scratch, spanning across real estate, strategic consulting, stressed asset management, buying and selling, lifestyle and retail. In 2014, he founded 360 Realtors, one of the largest real estate advisories in the country. He has been the brainchild behind 360 Rising Straits Management, an alternate investment fund (AIF) for stressed real estate assets. He has also founded Indsource, a leading buying agency focused on home and lifestyle products, and Rosemoore, a premium English home fragrance brand. Over the years, Ankit has built a reputation as a technology evangelist and a pioneer of forward-looking strategies. His acumen lies in identifying new business opportunities and building successful models around the same. At the same time, throughout his business journey, he has shown a strong commitment to maintaining high standards of integrity and customer convenience.

LESSON 9

BEING IN UNISON WITH GOVERNMENT GUIDELINES

In times such as this, when political leadership across the world kept implementing newer regulations every day, a significant proportion of which disrupted businesses, it could get frustrating to comply with some of these regulations. However, true leadership is when compliance is seen as a partnership; where organizations partner with authorities at various levels. Leadership is not just about complying with the regulations that are passed but also working with authorities in tuning these and then with all stakeholders (be it customers, suppliers, employees or even contractual labour) in ensuring compliance at the deepest levels. Leadership is also about enabling one's partner ecosystem in complying.

During lockdown, business leaders across different industries worked with the authorities in ensuring their essential workforce had the right approvals to move around. Mismatches between central and state authorities were frequently communicated and addressed. Instead of trying to point fingers and creating a me-versus-you scenario, leaders educated their staff on the importance of why these regulations were brought in the first place. Many trained their staff and changed their business processes to comply with the new guidelines. Many educated the authorities of their critical needs in order to serve their customers, especially those in the essential services.

This partnership ensured that despite the lockdown, movement of essential goods was not impacted. It also ensured safety was the guiding principle for one and all.

19

SHAPOORJI PALLONJI GROUP

The Shapoorji Pallonji Group has a rich legacy of 155 years, having been set up in 1865. It is a global, diversified business house that delivers end-to-end solutions in engineering and construction, infrastructure, real estate, water, energy, consumer products and financial services, among others. The group has a presence in over 70 countries across the world, with an employee base of over 70,000, and is committed to sustainable development.

The group derives a significant share of its business internationally, with a special emphasis on emerging markets, having ventured overseas as early as in the 1970s. Apart from India, it has a strong presence across business lines in the Middle East and Africa, and is now also present in Europe and the Americas.

Apart from the Shapoorji Pallonji mother brand, the other marquee brands of the group include AFCONS, Sterling and Wilson, Eureka Forbes, Forbes & Co. and Gokak Textiles.

The group has designed and built several civil, structural engineering and infrastructure landmarks in India and across the world, which serve millions and have aided development. It has delivered turnkey EPC (engineering, procurement and construction) solutions in oil and gas, power and renewable energy. It has gained worldwide recognition for its water and wastewater treatment solutions. In real estate, it has developed many of India's iconic skyscrapers, IT parks and affordable residences. The group also offers an integrated advisory platform for investments in the infrastructure and real estate sectors.

∼

Plans are nothing; planning is everything.

—Dwight D. Eisenhower

The COVID-19 crisis has impacted all organizations, large and small, irrespective of age, scale, industry or customer segment. Every organization is dealing with the crisis in its own way. So is the Shapoorji Pallonji Group, a 155-year-old highly respected business house; a global, diversified group with its presence in engineering and construction, infrastructure, real estate, energy, water, consumer durables and financial services, among others. The group has a presence in over 70 countries and has more than 70,000 employees.

The group is headquartered in Mumbai (Maharashtra), the epicentre of the pandemic in India. As we speak, the Maximum City, with a population of approx. 20 million has had around 70,000 cases by early July.

I am introduced to Shankar Krishnan, the head of strategy and information technology (IT) at the group. At the very beginning of our conversation, Shankar tells me how, in a large and diversified group like theirs, any experiences he would be sharing should be seen merely as a 'bird's-eye view'.

'All businesses within the Shapoorji Pallonji Group share the common values of the group. However, each business is empowered with the freedom to compete effectively in its industry. In such a diversified group, the impact of COVID-19 and the responses to deal with it, while common in several respects, have varied in certain ways across the different businesses of the group, and also across geographies,' Shankar says.

He adds, 'The sixth generation of the Mistry family is now actively involved in leading the group. However, even in such a long organizational memory, no event in our past comes close to this crisis, in its sheer complexity and impact.'

The group first noticed the direct impact of the COVID-19 crisis in late January 2020, due to disruptions in its supply chain for certain materials procured from China. However, the risks were then manageable.

'By mid-February, the crisis began to spread. Several countries beyond China started getting affected, including the Middle East, where some group businesses are present. Around half of our business is from overseas markets, and some of these geographies started seeing an impact on economic activity, including in our lines of work. Not every country was equally impacted; for instance, some countries in Africa were less affected, and had fewer restrictions, to begin with,' Shankar says.

He goes on to shed light on the steps the group took in the wake of the crisis. 'From the very beginning, we were clear that the first priority was to safeguard the health and safety of our employees and our extended work ecosystem. Being a globally spread-out group, several executives travel extensively. In early March, we proactively put in place stringent travel restrictions, both within a country and overseas. At the same time, senior HR executives of our group and its businesses collaborated to set in place guidelines and detailed work protocols for employee safety and health, leveraging best practice from within and outside our industries. This included protocols for our project sites, manufacturing locations and offices. While several guidelines were common, there was some flexibility across countries and businesses.

'Apart from this, the IT executives in the group collaborated to ensure preparedness for minimal disruption to critical business processes, to deal with the eventuality of most personnel having to work from home.'

In mid-March, the Government of India, learning from other countries, announced a country-wide lockdown. In the weeks that followed, there were stringent restrictions on the movement of people and materials. More than two-thirds of the group's business is from its core projects, particularly in engineering and construction and infrastructure; virtually all project sites in these businesses had to discontinue work. Needless to say, this was not something unique to the Shapoorji Pallonji Group, but its response surely was.

'Shapoorji Pallonji provided adequate food and provisions, and accommodation camps, to the labour deployed on all its project sites, to make it convenient for them to remain at site. We carried out regular health check-ups for the workforce and set up quarantine rooms inside labour camps to deal with suspect cases. The quality and adequacy of all camp services, such as drinking water, kitchens, washing areas and toilets, illumination, and waste collection and disposal, were regularly audited and actions taken to mitigate risks. Despite stoppage of work at project sites, we paid wages to the labour for several weeks into the shutdown. Additionally, there was open communication to the workforce on the issues at hand, and how the business was dealing with them, which helped in dispelling any panic reactions,' Shankar tells me.

'The construction industry is the second-largest employer in the country, after agriculture. It is a very people-intensive business. We are glad that we took utmost care of those who worked on our sites; we also believed that when the lockdown ended, this would help us restart operations without much delay.'

During the lockdown, the group's real estate division leveraged technology in all aspects of the business, including sales. It launched a campaign highlighting the importance of 'owning' a home, especially as recent times have had people spending more time with their families at home. They also launched a digital platform to provide a seamless home-buying experience. From providing Google Maps views to sample flat photographs, project-related information and master layout plans, the platform provided prospective customers with an actual site visit experience.

Some of the group's businesses, being essential services, continued to operate even during the lockdown. This included two ports (one on the east coast, and the other on the west coast), dealing with the import and export of critical commodities such as iron ore and coal. They followed strict protocol with respect to employee health and safety, to minimize risks even as operations were underway.

'Our two offshore oil and gas platforms in Bombay High, where we serve the Oil and Natural Gas Commission (ONGC), were also in the "essential services" category, helping to cater to the country's energy needs in this critical period. Our offshore personnel are typically rotated on a periodic basis to optimize productivity and provide them adequate time with their families. During the lockdown, it was not possible to rotate them with the same frequency as earlier, and they needed to stay on our vessels for a longer period. While essentials such as groceries and medical supplies were reaching the vessels regularly, the staff's morale and mental well-being were equally important. Our business leaders maintained a close and personal communication with them to build camaraderie and morale. In addition, they were provided free mobile and internet connectivity on a daily basis, for an extended time, so they could communicate with their families.'

Switching gears, we talk about Eureka Forbes, the group's flagship consumer goods business that sells water and air purifiers, vacuum cleaners and home security products. It is a market leader in the water segment and a household name, with brands such as Aquaguard under its banner. The business is based on in-home demonstrations and retail sales. A critical ingredient is its responsive 'service' workforce that caters to customer requests and complaints.

'Despite the need for water and pure air being a basic need, they were not listed as "essential services" during the lockdown. Any maintenance or repair of existing devices was not permitted. As the lockdown was extended, the backlog of service requests began to grow. We made sure our customers understood our limitations and the need to prioritize compliance and safety. We also worked with our channel partners in training the staff in safety protocols. As the restrictions eased, we prioritized serving existing customers over new sales and installations.

'One of the group's businesses, Forbes & Co., manufactures precision engineering products for the automotive and other industries. During the lockdown, leveraging its capabilities in engineering design and manufacturing, Forbes & Co. innovatively worked on developing a prototype for a breathing apparatus (akin to a ventilator), to assist in the current crisis. Interestingly, the entire design and prototyping were done by virtual collaboration, involving personnel working from their homes in different parts of the country.

'Gokak Textiles is our group company in the textiles business, with an integrated facility in Karnataka. Responding to the Government of India's call to domestic manufacturing enterprises to augment supply of critical items, it commenced manufacture of masks and PPE kits. It has supplied these products to state governments and other government institutions, apart from healthcare organizations.

'In all businesses of our group, there has been a realization of the power of digitization and virtual collaboration, and the criticality of a robust IT infrastructure and info-security to enable the same. Business leaders and managers have realized that while there is no substitute for face-to-face interaction in the world of work, there are several benefits of a "blended" model that combines real and virtual collaboration. This is a shift in mindset brought about by the current pandemic. It is a lesson we will leverage even in post-COVID times as we infuse a greater level of digitization and virtual collaboration into our day-to-day work, making it the "new normal".'

Looking ahead, Shankar believes that it will take a few months for the economy at large, and for businesses, to come back on track. Thankfully, ever since partial or phased 'unlock' has commenced, the trend has been positive, with economic activity picking up week on week.

Shankar suggests that to emerge from the crisis, it is imperative for the Government of India to 'pump-prime' the economy, by setting out the road map for infrastructure projects in various themes and by enabling the same. This would have a large 'multiplier effect' on the economy, and will also help employment generation. These themes should include public health infrastructure (such as hospitals and allied healthcare centres), which has emerged as a crying need for our nation.

'It is quite likely that there will be a fundamental "reset" of global supply chains in many industries, as businesses start thinking of ways and means to reduce their overdependence on China. This would have far-reaching implications for India, benefiting the manufacturing, logistics and infrastructure segments. However, it calls for businesses to proactively recalibrate and pivot their strategies to capitalize on this shift.'

Shankar concludes by saying that he is optimistic about the future; he is confident that the inherent resilience of the Shapoorji Pallonji Group, and the capabilities of its various businesses, would enable it to leverage these shifts as the world slowly but surely moves to the post-COVID phase in the months ahead.

About Shankar Krishnan

Shankar Krishnan is Group Head, Strategy and IT, Shapoorji Pallonji Group.

He works in close coordination with the promoters, his peers in the Group Centre, and the leadership teams of the businesses, to drive the group's strategic growth agenda. This includes institutionalization of processes related to strategy formulation and implementation, as also assistance in the incubation of new businesses within the group.

Additionally, Shankar oversees the teams involved in IT for the group, which include IT application development and support, digitization, IT infrastructure and info-security.

Shankar also serves on the Boards and Management Boards of select companies and business divisions of the group.

Prior to joining the Shapoorji Pallonji Group, Shankar worked for more than 15 years in the management consulting practice of Accenture, where he worked with clients in diverse industries in India, the Middle East and Southeast Asia, in the areas of business strategy, organizational change management, operational improvement and IT strategy.

Shankar graduated with a B.E (Honors) in civil engineering

from VJTI (Mumbai University) and was a recipient of the J.N. Tata Endowment scholarship. He then obtained an MBA at the Indian Institute of Management Ahmedabad (IIMA).

Shankar's interests include reading, music, quizzing, table tennis and travelling.

20

EMERSON

Emerson was established in 1890 in St. Louis, Missouri as Emerson Electric Manufacturing Co. by Civil War Union veteran John Wesley Emerson to manufacture electric motors using a patent owned by the Scottish-born brothers Charles and Alexander Meston. In 1892, it became the first brand to sell electric fans in the United States (US). It quickly expanded its product line to include electric sewing machines, electric dental drills and power tools. Emerson concentrates on the most complex, profound challenges facing the world in the process, industrial, commercial and residential markets. Emerson's global talent, best-in-class technologies and core platforms deliver value across a range of industries and sectors. With Emerson, you can always Consider It Solved™.

Established in 1997, the Emerson Export Engineering Center was the company's first global engineering centre to be set up outside the US. The centre presently has a workforce strength of over 1,650 employees who service Emerson's global network of customers. The centre supports various business verticals of Emerson's Automation Solution platform and provides various project services.

∼

Automation won't take your job, but the self-inflicted imprisonment of industrial isolation will.

—Richie Norton

In a time when the entire world is waiting for a vaccine for this pandemic, I was curious to understand how mass production of a drug works. It isn't just about the raw chemical ingredients but about mixing them in the right proportion, keeping the formulation at the right temperature, making capsules out of the same, packaging, distribution and complying to the Food and Drug Administration's (FDA) and other agencies' regulations. Each of these steps is critical to the manufacturing and supply chain. Each step in manufacturing needs not just humans but also equipment, machines and other resources. The amount of raw material to be added, the amount of heat to be supplied, the time of settling—each of the steps here needs to be timely and highly precise. And achieving this at scale is incredibly hard without industrial automation.

During my research about industrial automation, I learnt the importance of this otherwise obscure industry in our lives. Seemingly simple parameters such as temperature, pressure, flow, density, levels, etc. are extremely critical to varied industries. It does not matter if you are running a pharmaceutical plant or a power plant, a fertilizer plant or doing oil and gas exploration. Processes around temperature, pressure and flow measurement, corrosion monitoring, flame and gas detection, density and viscosity checks not just keep the plants operational but also safe. Emerson's automation solutions provide several products and services to take care of all of these efficiently and reliably.

I reached out to Ravindra Agrawal, director at Emerson's engineering centre in Pune, for understanding what has been the impact of this crisis on the automation industry. Ravindra has been with Emerson for the last 20 years, supporting global offices in pre-sales to commissioning of automation solutions for various industries.

The company started seeing the early trends in China and started calling its Indian workforce back to the home locations.

'Automation projects are complex and need skilled manpower at the plant locations. Right from commissioning to training the client over the management and monitoring of the automation system need onsite support.

'A typical solution design and deployment entail customizing the products for the client and deploying at the client site. Offshore employees simulate the client configuration on the hardware in their own office's premise. Once fully tested as part of FAT (Factory Acceptance Test), the configuration is deployed at the client's location by the onshore workforce.'

In business-to-business industries such as these, large client projects are long-term business relationships. Besides, the clients themselves are in critical services to their customers. Pulling out people in an unplanned manner would have not only dented Emerson's relationship with the client but also disrupted their businesses. What came to Emerson's rescue was the availability of a distributed workforce, both in terms of their skill set and presence across the globe, early adoption of newer technologies and robust processes.

'Over the past 15 years, Emerson has developed and deployed a global sourcing and manufacturing strategy ensuring operational redundancies are in place to minimize disruptions in our ability to deliver products and solutions for our client's needs. Despite the challenges we are seeing across the automation industry, this strategy is enabling us to maintain customer support, production and delivery levels with minimal interruption in all global regions.

'We quickly reached out to every individual employee, be it offshore or at locations back home, through their supervisors. A cadence was set to understand challenges, health status and connectivity status for every individual. At management meetings, we discussed every project requirement and deliberated on possibilities to support by moving resources, swapping resources or even supporting remotely with shift working. We have managed most of the critical support requests and maintained our overall customer satisfaction.

'Rebalancing was also done across industries. The oil and gas sector was experiencing a downturn due to low oil prices and many projects were postponed and few even cancelled. The demand for power was also low at this time when industries were under lockdowns in a large part of the globe. Similarly, summers in Europe meant less need for fuel for heating. Shutdown in large parts of the globe meant lower demand for oil and gas. At the same time, pharmaceutical projects were extremely critical and on an accelerated path. We moved manpower from groups supporting power, oil and gas to pharmaceutical and medical devices.

'Each such decision was taken being fully transparent to our clients and in conjunction with them. The clients too were not untouched by the crisis and were supportive in partnering in the best possible support that could be provided under such circumstances.'

Besides the manpower, availability of critical hardware and spare parts for its products also became a challenge. Emerson's Lifecycle Services Program helps in maintaining the required level of support for any and all after Service Support. The programme has a tiered approach. Customized offerings are given based on the location and complexity of the project.

Emerson's leadership was quick to realize that this crisis needed a longer-term horizon and needed a major rethinking of manpower-intensive tasks for its clients. Not only was the availability of manpower a challenge, their safety was of utmost importance.

'All the industries have their KPI (Key Performance Indices) linked to overall Productivity, Safety, Reliability and Emission. Emerson framed the Operation Certainty Program for the same. In an industrial environment, if something does break, that results in not just production or quality disruption but can even result in an accident or someone being killed. So when we talk about our solutions, we're really thinking about the impact on KPIs,' Ravindra explains.

Site surveys to do a health monitoring of the plant machinery are a daily routine for all industries, but need skilled and specialized manpower to understand the health, performance and safety of the machinery and take the appropriate control measures.

'We began with simple remote monitoring wherein the need of specialized manpower was minimized. Clients could deploy unskilled people to take visual shots of the site, including the parameters of the assets/machine. Voice, written and video instructions were given to these people, in order to be able to execute the monitoring without needing to understand it deeply.

Emerson developed virtual capabilities in the automation industry for clients to leverage and minimize their team's travel and exposure. These include cloud engineering, Virtual Factory Acceptance Tests, the availability of MyEmerson digital tools (to engineer solutions, manage installed assets, streamline procurement processes and access online training), and the ability to support, both technically and commercially, through remote collaboration and virtual meeting capabilities.'

The need of the hour has pushed the acceptance of drones, augmented reality (AR) based virtual monitoring and similar innovative solutions. Robotic management of control rooms were being explored before the crisis. But the COVID crisis has accelerated the path to the acceptances of such innovations.

With collaborative robots, which make up the fastest-growing robotics market, the robot becomes almost like your avatar. They give the ability to actually control some of the processes that you're responsible for in the plant, even if you're not physically there.

'Many manufacturers are increasing efforts to equip their human workers with digital connected-worker tools that incorporate safety checks into workflows, ensure collaboration with colleagues when physical contact is off the cards and other such processes that ultimately balance business continuity and employee health. This is also the dawn of a new era where front-line workers and desk workers are harmonized with tools that can support the flow of collaboration and data, and even event triggers, where something that happens on the factory floor initiates a communication or workflow in the back office.

'And although the concept of using connected-worker technology to empower workers around safety, quality and productivity may be heightened right now, it will still be just as critical to build business resiliency after this pandemic is over.

'Clients are now excited to invest in such solutions whose value goes beyond the immediate crisis,' Ravindra tells me.

In times when the pandemic will force a redesign of the industrial plants, the leadership at Emerson is looking at a seamless and cost-efficient transition for all its clients. Be it remote support and surveillance with minimal need of skilled supervision or ensuring its own products face minimal supply chain disruptions due to reliance on fewer supply partners, the company understands the criticality of its existence for its clients.

As Ravindra succinctly puts it, 'We exist because our clients do. And in times like these, we are not thinking in a typical provider-client relationship mode, but as equal partners. And as we lead through this crisis, we have the needs of our client's customers in mind.'

About Ravindra Agrawal

Ravindra Agrawal, director (projects), is an Instrumentation and Control engineering graduate from the College of Engineering Pune (COEP). He started his professional career with Ballarpur Industries and led the automation of their Rishikesh and Pune glass plants. He set up a small-sized instrumentation contracting firm to support various Thermax projects across India.

Ravindra joined Siemens in 1998 and relocated to Delhi, he managed many R&M (Renovation and Modernization) jobs for Siemens, including DPL (Durgapur Power), APGENCO (Kothagudem) and Sriram Fertilizers (Kota), to name few.

Ravindra has been with Emerson since 1 November 2000 and has held various capacity roles at its locations globally. He managed Proman GmbH's ammonia plant, the methanol programme based out of Germany. In 2007, he moved to Emerson's Middle East and Africa (MEA) headquarter at Jebel Ali in Dubai and managed many marquee accounts in Programme manager capacity such as Qatar Gas, Petroleum Development of Oman (PDO).

Ravindra is currently located in Emerson's Pune Engineering Centre and responsible for supporting all digital transformation pursuits and projects.

LESSON 10

IMPORTANCE OF TECHNOLOGY

One widely observed feature of the COVID-19 pandemic has been how it has accelerated and magnified pre-existing trends within society and the global economy. One of these is the increase in adoption of technology as part of the company's DNA.

Who would have believed if someone had predicted that the whole world will be working from home for such a long time? Forget just the core software industry, a significant proportion of non-IT employees are also working from home today.

Who would have imagined buying one's dream home virtually? How about demo and maintenance of large industrial plants through completely automated systems, which need minimal physical supervision? How about digital channels to reach directly to one's customers, bypassing levels of intermediaries?

In a crisis, one of the most critical priorities is ensuring employees can access critical systems from home, customers can get in touch with the company and all stakeholders can have access to the necessary data required to do their jobs. This also involves re-engineering of not just business processes and IT systems but also security and reliability systems to ensure minimal downtimes and risks of hacking and data leakages.

Supply chain innovations led by augmented reality are paving the way for converting the traditional face-to-face delivery models to virtual deliveries, remote set-ups and monitoring. Redesigning core platforms to handle downtimes without dependency on human intervention is the key to de-risking business continuity during a crisis.

Irrespective of one's industry, scale or geography, the crisis has led leaders to heavily focus and invest in the technology. Leaders play a critical role in narrowing the divide between business' understanding of technology's strategic value and the actual importance of the same. Businesses across industries need infrastructure to support digital connectivity, storage and processing power. This includes the fixed-line fibre optic networks that transmit internet communications to businesses and homes, as well as the data centres that offer storage and computation on demand, playing the same role to data-intensive businesses that the national grid does to energy-intensive ones. Capital flows into these assets needs to grow exponentially.

Even when people begin to get back to work, leaders will need to invest in technologies to monitor and protect employee health, ensure sanitization and social distancing. The internet of things ecosystem will become crucial in aggregating and analysing all of the inputs across several sensor devices at workplaces.

Adoption of automation, virtual processes and remote working is not just an infrastructural challenge but rather a mindset shift that needs to happen from the highest to the lowest ladders of the organization.

CONCLUSION

A lot has changed since I wrote the first story of this book. Our worlds have shrunk to our homes. Our lives have been impacted in unimaginable ways forever. Some of us, including myself, have had our near and dear ones suffer this disease. We have been up, close and personal with its impacts, in more ways than one. Some losses are forever. At the same time, this period has seen innovations like never before. Competing companies are coming together and forming symbiotic partnerships.

In my journey of writing this book, at times I felt that leadership was meaningless when we all are confronted constantly with the thought of mortality. At other times, these leaders and their spirits kept my hopes high and taught me that leadership can never be more important than it is now. And the onus of leadership lies with each one of us. We all need to lead ourselves, our loved ones, our societies, organizations and countries out of this and every crisis.

As I hand over the manuscript to the publisher, I have formed a personal bond with these leaders. I hope these organizations keep going strong and are not faced with tough choices.

The journey of writing a book during this pandemic, of interviewing, researching and writing while also thinking of the next meeting at work or the dirty dishes in the sink has been a memorable one.

Hope you enjoyed and learnt from this journey. I will love to hear from you at dreamerdisha@gmail.com

ACKNOWLEDGEMENTS

Gratitude to the leaders who gave me their valuable time for the interviews and the multiple edits. Thank you for opening up and sharing the valuable lessons and being so candid.

Gratitude to my family for all the support and being part of the journey. Thank you, Hubby, for staying up with me, so I did not feel lazy to write; for all the tea you made for me.

Gratitude to the friends who introduced me to these leaders. In your busy lives, you prioritized my request for connections and introduced me in words that left the leaders interested in being part of this book.

Gratitude to the readers for taking out your precious time and believing this book can be a worthy read. In a world of so many distractions, muster this attention is no mean feat. I hope you enjoy the journey of reading.

Gratitude to the readers of my previous books. Every email I get in my inbox on how one of my previous books touched your life gives writing a purpose in my life.

Gratitude to Rupa Publications for helping this work take the shape of a book. In times of lockdowns, co-creating a new book and making sure it reaches the readers is extremely challenging.

Gratitude to the Almighty. I am nothing without you.

INDEX

Aarogya Setu, 26
Aashirvaad Box of Hope, 9
AatmaNirbhar, 137, 165
Action COVID-19 Team (Act), 28
active pharmaceutical ingredients (APIs), 17
Airbnb, 119
allied healthcare centres, 176
All India Institute of Medical Sciences (AIIMS), 52
Amazon, 125, 134
Anti-viral disinfection, 73
artificial intelligence, 33, 75, 87, 115, 122
assets under management (AUM), 30
augmented reality, 40, 183, 188
automation industry, 180, 181, 183

Bengaluru police, 36
bike taxi, 80
Bill & Melinda Gates Foundation, 28
Blind Relief Association, 101
border issues, 54
boutique properties, 74
business-as-usual, 89
business continuity plan, v, 77, 79

Central Government Health Scheme (CGHS), 17
Charles and Alexander Meston, 179

China, 7, 17, 58, 70, 117, 120, 160, 165, 173, 177, 180
Citizenship Amendment Bill (CAB), 51
cloud engineering, 183
collaborative robots, 183
connected-worker technology, 183
contactless check-ins, 73
contactless delivery, 149
contact tracing, 28
containment zones, 46, 63, 65, 101
corporate gifting, 98
Crime Branch, 42
cross-disability organization, 98
cybercrimes, 46

data-backed trading, 33
dedicated fever clinics, 14
deep tech domain, 115
Defence Research and Development Organisation (DRDO), 136
demand forecasting, 80
de-risking business continuity, 188
digital coaching, 142
digital health records, 123, 127
Digital India, 161
Digitalization, 55
Digital upgradation, 166
drones, 183

Economic Offence Wing, 42

e-coupon, 100
e-education, 118
E-grocers, 82
emergency response communication, 122, 127
employee health, 174, 183, 189
employee safety, 4, 33, 62, 103, 173
EnCloudEn, 118
E-Prop Show, 162
e-site visits, 163
Ethereal Machines, 28

Feed The Needy, 155
Fibre-based networks, 64
FOD, 98
front-line workers, 9, 17, 45, 55, 96, 183

gamification, 116
GiveIndia, 99
Google, 40, 78, 80, 81, 148, 174
Google Maps, 40, 174

Hapag-Lloyd, 69
headcount reduction, 120
health insurance, 26
heat-sensing, 73
high-touch business, 63
Hike Messenger, 86
hoarding, viii, 82
Home isolation, 46
Hoppr, 86
Horticultural Producers Co-operative Marketing and Processing Society (HOPCOMS), 109
Hotstar, 8

hyperlocal deliveries, 6

illiquid penny stocks, 34
Incentive Travel, 69
Indian Council of Medical Research (ICMR), 26, 52, 54
Indsource International, 160
industrial automation, 180
info-security, 176, 177
infrastructural challenge, 189
Infrastructure Leasing & Financial Services (IL&FS), 159
infusion package, 164
internet-of-things (IoT), 115, 122
isolation centres, 45, 52
ITC e-Choupal 4.0, 8

Janaagraha, 121
Janata curfew, 51, 108

Karvy mega scam, 34
KITE, 30

Landmark Forum, 139, 140, 143
Lightbox, 80
liquidity crisis, 164

machine learning, 75, 115, 122
Make in India, 6
medical tourism, 17
metal disinfectants, 149
micro-entrepreneurs, 22
migrant labour camps, 66
Milkbasket, 40
mindset shift, 189
Mission Shakti, 24
movement stickers, 83

MyEmerson digital tools, 183
myresQR Sanitizer Refill Services, 125

National Accreditation Board for Hospitals & Healthcare Providers (NABH), 11
National Accreditation Board for Testing and Calibration Laboratories (NABL), 11
New Delhi Municipal Council (NDMC), 45
Nifty, 34

odd–even formula, 54
online gaming, 118
online retail, 118
Ookla, 66
Operation Certainty Program, 182
over-the-top (OTT), 60
oxygen concentrators, 111

package holiday providers, 70
payout time, 83
Paytm, 34
pharmaceutical projects, 182
PM CARES Fund, 8
Pristyn Care, 26
provider-client relationship mode, 184
pump-prime, 176

quarantine management, 28

Rainmatter, 30, 37
real estate industry, 159, 160
real estate media, 159
Rebalancing, 181
red zones, 63, 100
remote working, 159, 165, 189
repo rate, 154, 164
restructuring, 72
Reverse migration, 165
ring-fencing, 84
Rise for Restaurants, 155
RIU Protect, 73
Robotic management, 183

sensor devices, 189
shift working, 181
Smart Dispenser traQR, 125
social distancing, 149
social media handles, 153
Special Police Unit for Women and Children (SPUWAC), 42
staggered boarding, 73
Sunfeast Box of Happiness, 9
Swasthaadhaar, 123, 127

Tablighi Jamaat, 53
tele-consultation, 13, 47
touchpoint, 33, 62, 66, 160
transformative education, 144
transgenders, 126
travel e-commerce, 74

Unnati, 98
unorganized labour, 28

venture capitalists, 116
virtual cash, 155
virtual collaboration, 176
Virtual Factory Acceptance Tests, 183

Virtual Reality, 115, 162

Wadhwani Foundation, 28
walk-in customer, 83
warehouse space, 166
war widows, 126
wastewater treatment solutions, 171
webinars, 162

WhatsApp, 80, 86, 107, 153
Wi-Fi hotspots, 66
work from home (WFH), 119

Yatra, 70, 75
Yulu, 116, 148

Zoom, 35, 161

Made in the USA
Monee, IL
03 May 2026